To:

From:

THE WONDER OF GOD'S GRACE

Published in 2009 by Struik Christian Gifts
An imprint of Struik Christian Media
A division of New Holland Publishing (South Africa) (Pty) Ltd
(New Holland Publishing is a member of Avusa Ltd)
Cornelis Struik House
80 McKenzie Street
Cape Town 8001

Reg. No. 1971/009721/07

Project management by Reinata Thirion
Translation by Lizel Grobbelaar
Edited by Inge du Plessis
DTP by Sonja Louw
Images by stock.xpert
Cover design by Sonja Louw
Cover image by stock.xpert
Printed and bound by China Translation and Printing
Services Ltd, Hong Kong

ISBN 978-1-4153-0654-3

www.struikchristianmedia.co.za

The
Wonder
of
God's
Grace

NINA SMIT

SCG
STRUIK CHRISTIAN GIFTS

Contents

[This grace] has now been revealed by the appearing of our Savior Jesus Christ, who has abolished death and brought life and immortality to light through the gospel ...

— 2 Timothy 1:10

The Wonder of God's Grace

A Lesson at Easter

We will never be able to comprehend the grace God has bestowed upon humankind — it will always remain a mystery. However, if we have faith in Jesus, we may receive it with both hands. In one of his books, the writer Arthur Gordon shares a precious lesson he learnt at Easter. His father had encouraged him and his sister to put part of their pocket-money in a piggy bank throughout the year. The piggy banks were then opened at Easter and the money given to charity. This gesture was intended to help them to understand that we should be prepared to give to others because God gave us his Son. Gordon writes that he always badly needed the money soon after he had dropped it into his piggy bank. He would therefore 'rob' his piggy bank so that it used to be practically empty by Easter, whereas his sister's piggy bank would be chock-a-block. One year his Aunt Daisy visited the family at Easter and she was present when the piggy banks were opened. As usual Arthur's piggy bank was almost empty and his sister's full. Aunt Daisy offered to fill Arthur's piggy bank, but his sister was upset about this suggestion. 'That's not fair,' she muttered. 'You're right,' Aunt Daisy said. 'It's not fair, but God does not treat us fairly, He is a God of grace. I believe that God Himself will one day reward you for your faithfulness.' Arthur's dad was not happy about the situation either – and Aunt Daisy then asked him whether he had ever received an undeserved gift before. Then she turned to Arthur and said, 'Arthur, always remember that God loves you very much, but don't push Him too far!' Not only did he never rob his piggy bank again, says Gordon, but he also realised the meaning of God's grace in practice for the first time.

God's Grace Is for You

God still offers all humankind his grace and mercy. Every-body sins and deserves the death penalty, but God never judges us according to what we deserve; He has mercy on us. He removes every vestige of sin if we believe in Jesus. Colossians 2:14 says, '[He has] wiped out the handwriting of requirements that was against us, which was contrary to us. And He has taken it out of the way, having nailed it to the cross.' The consequence of God's grace in your life and mine is therefore that we have now been set free from sin for all eternity. Faith in Jesus Christ is the door to God's grace. 'Therefore, having been justified by faith, we have peace with God through our Lord Jesus Christ, through whom also we have access by faith into this grace in which we stand, and rejoice in hope of the glory of God. And not only that, but we also glory in tribulations, knowing that tribulation produces per-severance,' Paul says to the church in Rome (Rom 5:1–3).

It will always remain a miracle that God wants to share the glory of his grace as well as heaven with us. We should therefore make time to rejoice about this. However, God's grace does not take away all the suffering in your life. The suffering that God at times permits in your life is not intended to destroy your blessed assurance of God's grace. In fact, it serves as a test to reinforce your assurance. And God Himself is the foundation of this assurance of his grace! 'The assurance that God is God, is also your assurance that you will share in his glory,' we read in the *Bybellennium*.

It is as simple as this: God offers you his grace free of charge, provided you have faith in Jesus, and because He does this, you can have the wonderful hope that you will one day be in heaven!

Heavenly Father,

You are merciful and gracious; patient and loving.
I cannot grasp your grace toward me —
thank you that I do not have to understand it —
that I merely have to accept it in gratitude.
Lord, I know that your grace is sufficient for me;
that your mercy never comes to an end
and that it is revealed to me by Jesus
who has destroyed the power of death,
so that I will one day live in heaven for ever.
Thank you that I may approach
your throne of grace with boldness,
to receive the gift of your grace at the right time.
Help me to have mercy on others,
because You are so merciful to me.

God Himself is mercy. He is with me:
In illness. At the grave of a loved one.
Anywhere and everywhere, and
whenever I am lonely and helpless and
dependent. Grace is the ability to see, sense,
experience God in my circumstances.
Grace does not remove threatening
circumstances, but provides a brand new
perspective on such circumstances.
Grace does not paint over the darkness in
my circumstances, but touches it with God's
unwavering love and faithfulness.
Grace is to start exploiting the wealth of God's
love, which reinforces every situation, regardless
of the apparent hopelessness. It is the perspective
of grace here on the level road for those who have
already discovered the way of grace
which leads to heaven.

– Johan Smit

If you would ... stretch out your hands toward Him ... you could be steadfast, and not fear; because you would forget your misery, and remember it as waters that have passed away, and your life would be brighter than noonday. Though you were dark, you would be like the morning.

—Job 11:13, 16–17

Blueprint for Happiness

On the Sunday after the well-known singer Taliep Pietersen had been murdered, one of our ministers wrote the following anonymous quotation on the PowerPoint of our congregation:

> Work — as if you do not need money;
> Dance — as if no-one is watching you;
> Sing — as if no-one is listening to you;
> Love — as if you have never been hurt;
> Live — as if we already have heaven on earth.

Before and after the service, the conversations of church members were fairly pessimistic — we were all wondering how long the ever-soaring spiral of violence would continue before radical measures would be taken to counter it. Back home I took my ever-present little notebook from my bag and studied the quotation again. It struck me that, should everybody in South Africa follow this advice, the situation in our country — and in our lives — would change dramatically.

Heaven on Earth!

Would you like to reflect on this quotation with me?

Working — most of us work without much enthusiasm. We try to earn the maximum amount of money with the least effort — but, as you know, work is a necessary evil because we cannot survive without money! Suppose we worked because we love and enjoy it, because what we do is our passion ... Suppose we followed the golden rule of the Preacher: Whatever your hand finds to do, do it with all your might ... Suppose we always put God above Mammon so that money and possessions were no longer of supreme importance to us?

Dancing — I had to smile about this requirement because both my husband and I were born with two left feet. However, it would be rather wonderful to dance without any inhibitions, like David danced before the ark. To dance merely because you enjoy it and because you want to praise the Lord with your whole being. Just as the ark was the sign of God's presence to David — hence his exuberance — God's presence in the lives of his children should still bring joy to them.

Singing — I have a problem singing in church, particularly when the melody is complicated and only a few people are singing. Not only do I have two left feet, but instead of singing I can only drone. And I do *so* love singing! If I could sing when no-one was within earshot or note my discordant droning, I would definitely sing at the top of my voice in church (and in the shower!).

Loving — It's natural to love those close to you, but unfortunately not everybody is easy to love. Those who have been hurt before are also very wary of loving again. CS Lewis said that if you wish to avoid pain it is better not to love at all, because love is invariably accompanied by pain. However, Jesus commands us to love one another, and the Holy Spirit in us enables us to love. Paul says in Romans, 'The love of God has been poured out in our hearts by the Holy Spirit who was given to us' (Rom 5:5).

Living as if we already have heaven on earth — Despite the current negative conditions in our country, this is still possible because if you love God, heaven is already within you, and not somewhere in the distant future, after death.

Decide right now, with me, to try to live according to the instructions given in this anonymous quotation.

If you do, you will indeed experience heaven on earth!

Lord,

I want to be happy —
I no longer want to be pessimistic about the future.
Please help me to be happy from now on:
To work as if I do not need money;
to dance as if no-one is watching me;
to sing as if no-one is listening to me;
to love as if I have never been hurt before;
to live as if heaven is already on earth.
However, to do this I need You in my life.
Help me to do all things to your glory,
to radiate the inner joy You give
by the way I act and speak.
Help me to love others
with the same unconditional love
with which You love me —
so that heaven will indeed be created around me
even though I still reside on earth.

If I had my life to live over,
I'd relax. I would limber up.
I would take fewer things seriously ...
I would climb more mountains
and swim more rivers.
If I had to do it over again,
I would travel lighter than I have.
I would start barefoot earlier in the spring
and stay that way later in the fall.
I would go to more dances.
I would ride more merry-go-rounds
and I would pick more daisies.

– Anonymous

The works of the Lord are great,
studied by all who have pleasure in them.
His work is honorable and glorious, and
His righteousness endures forever.

– Psalm 111:2–3

A World Filled with God

A World Filled with Miracles

When we carefully look at the world around us, we cannot fail to see that it is filled to overflowing with the miracles of God; what is more, it is filled with God Himself. 'The world is crowded with Him. He walks everywhere incognito. And the incognito is not always easy to penetrate. The real labor is to remember to attend. In fact to come awake. Still more to remain awake.' This is what CS Lewis wrote to a fictitious friend in his well-known book: *Letters to Malcolm, Chiefly on Prayer.*

It is possible to see the world in a grain of sand and the heavens in a wild flower, the English poet William Blake rightly said.

We see evidence of God all around us. Miracles that shock us into recognising God's incomparable greatness and majesty. Those who look at the world and God in this way, are once again amazed at his absolutely incomprehensible grace and love poured out on us.

I can remember several such shocks in my own life when I suddenly had a crystal-clear vision of God: A bitterly cold night in Sutherland when the stars were so bright and seemed so close that I could practically touch them; a night when we heard mindboggling statistics about the heavens at the observatory. It is incredible that our galaxy is but one of millions of galaxies — and that some are so far away that their light has not even reached us yet. Then there was an overcast day in the Lake District in England when the sun suddenly broke through the heavy cloud cover and a perfect double rainbow spanned the green hills. The incessant rain of the previous two days was almost worthwhile to have seen this miracle. One evening when my husband and I went for a walk along the beach as usual, the sunset was an absolutely unreal glory of red, orange and yellow. The clouds were mirrored in a golden-red glow on the sea and on the wet sand under our feet. The whole world was golden and red and orange and we were right in the middle of it all. Had I seen a painting of this scene I would not have believed the unparalleled combination of colours. We sat on the beach until the sun disappeared behind the sea and the world around us was dark, but both of us still remember this specific walk with photographic clarity. Another time we were hiking through the Knysna Forest when we suddenly came upon a gossamery cobweb between two giant trees. The sunlight which lit it from behind had turned it into a silver filigree — it was incredible that the work of art had been created by a mere spider!

Then there were the moments after the birth of each of our three children, when the doctor placed a perfect, tiny baby in my arms and I experienced a new kind of love stirring in me. So, too, the wonder whenever I take a grandchild in my arms for the first time.

We were able to photograph some of these miraculous moments – like the double rainbow and the picturesque sunset. Others have been engraved in my memories for ever. However, when I think about these glimpses of God in my own life, I'm always amazed at how great God is!

Deeds Filled with Majesty and Splendour

The works of the Lord are great, writes the psalmist. His deeds are majestic and splendid. Do you still notice God's majestic and splendid deeds? Do you make time in your busy daily schedule to consider his deeds? Unless you are finely tuned to notice these glimpses of God in nature, you will easily miss them. And when this happens, you miss so much. Can you share similar pictures in your own life which reminded you intensely of God's presence? Or are you so fast asleep that you no longer notice God's miracles around you? If you cannot recall a number of these moments of awe, it is time to wake up and be alert so you will not miss another miracle and fail to recognise God. And if, like me, you can testify about several appointments with God in nature, remember to thank Him for them, and to remember them often with gratitude.

Lord,

thank you for the numerous times
when I have seen your fingerprints around me in nature,
when I could see You Yourself in the
incredibly beautiful world You have created.
Thank you for giving us glowing sunsets
and wonderful rainbows, delicate cobwebs
and bright stars to fill us with wonder;
things which once again remind us of your greatness.
I stand amazed that You Who created all these wonders
know me personally and love me.
Help me to be aware of the beauty around me every day —
that I will never simply pass by your beauty
without kneeling speechlessly before your majesty.
Help me also to see every fragment of individual beauty
as You Yourself, and never to stop praising
and glorifying You.

The more familiar I become with nature,
the closer I study the tiniest flower,
and see butterflies and insects dancing
merrily on aromatic herbs, the more
I believe in an incredible miracle.
I discover endless surprises
and am absolutely convinced
that a fragment of paradise
is presented to us here on earth.

— Phil Bosmans

The Lord is merciful and gracious, slow to anger, and abounding in mercy... For as the heavens are high above the earth, so great is His mercy toward those who fear Him ...But the mercy of the Lord is from everlasting to everlasting ...

– Psalm 103:8, 11, 17

What Love Does

A Love Such as God's

God's love for his children is immeasurably great, absolutely everlasting and totally incomprehensible. It is quite frightening to realise that Jesus asks us to love one another as He loves us. In fact, He says, 'A new commandment I give to you, that you love one another; as I have loved you, that you also love one another. By this all will know you are My disciples, if you have love for one another' (John 13:34–35).

Love does three things, John Ortberg says in his book, *Love Beyond Reason:*

- You are always on the side of the person you love;
- love rejoices in and enjoys the beloved; and
- love is prepared to give and serve.

These three features of love come to the fore in God's relationship with his children in a surprising way!

God Is on Your Side

Paul writes to the Christians in Rome: 'What then shall we say to these things? If God is for us, who can be against us? He who did not spare His own Son, but delivered Him up for us all, how shall He not with Him also freely give us all things?' (Rom 8:31–32).

God is always on your side. He has your interests at heart, His love for you is so vast that He did not even spare his own Son, but gave Him so that you could be saved. He cares for you and bears you up throughout your life. God is for you, therefore nothing and nobody can actually be against you. With Him you will always be more than a conqueror.

God Rejoices over You

The second feature of love is that it rejoices over and enjoys the beloved. Before the relationship between God and man was sullied by Adam and Eve's disobedience, God rejoiced over His creation — He Himself said that everything He had made was 'very good' (see Genesis 1:31).

Even after the Fall He still rejoiced over His children. 'The LORD your God in your midst, the Mighty One, will save; He will rejoice over you with gladness, He will quiet you in His love, He will rejoice over you with singing' (Zeph 3:17).

However, when mankind rejected God's love, we read that God 'was sorry that He had made man on the earth, and He was grieved in His heart' (Gen 6:6). It is therefore your responsibility to live and act in such a way that God will always rejoice over you.

A Love that Serves

Thirdly, love is prepared to give and to serve. This feature of love once again perfectly reflects God's love for us. He sacrifices his only Son so that everyone who believes in Him will never perish but have eternal life. He sends Jesus into the world to die the cruellest death imaginable because He loves us so much — and so that we can be delivered from all our sins through Jesus' death on Calvary. Unconditional love is indeed giving without expecting anything in return.

God's love is also prepared to serve. Jesus Himself says that He had not come to be served but to serve, and to give his life as ransom for many (see Matthew 20:28). Jesus' whole life is truly characterised by service. He was always helping people, touching and healing them. He even raised people from the dead.

If you are really prepared to live the love of God you will also have to be prepared to comply with these three characteristics of love: You will have to choose to be on the side of those you love, to rejoice over them, and to be prepared to give of yourself and serve them.

Heavenly Father,

thank you for your love for me —
a love I cannot fathom or explain;
but a love I accept with tremendous gratitude;
a love that is always on my side;
that rejoices over me and enjoys me,
a love that is prepared to give unconditionally,
and to give and serve wholeheartedly for my sake.
I would like to echo this love in my own life, Lord.
Please enable me to love like You.
Help me always to be prepared to be on the side
of those I love;
to rejoice over them and enjoy them;
to give myself to them unconditionally
and to be prepared to serve them.
I ask this in the Name of your Son
Who demonstrated this love to me.

Love goes deeper than skin-deep;
love makes itself at home and stays
voluntarily in the unknown rooms of
someone else's thoughtlife. Love looks carefully,
thinks unhurriedly, considers and reconsiders
judgements and verdicts before they are
verbalised. I can live without people,
but not without the love of a person.

– Maretha Maartens

That which was from the beginning, which we have heard, which we have seen with our eyes, which we have looked upon, and our hands have handled, concerning the Word of life... truly our fellowship is with the Father and with His Son Jesus Christ.

— 1 John 1:1, 3b

The Gentle Touch of God

Touch Is Important

The disciples of Jesus were truly privileged. While He was with them, they saw Him 'with their eyes', they heard his voice and touched Him 'with their hands'. They also experienced his touch.

Physical touch is important to all of us. Doctors have discovered that premature babies who are picked up and cuddled have a much better chance to survive than those who are not. By touch we indicate that we care and love one another.

It's very special to me when my husband gives me a bear hug, or when my grandchildren get a stranglehold on my neck, and when my eldest son returns from abroad and lifts me up and swings me. I love holding the latest grandchild in my arms and feeling the soft down on his little head against my cheek, or hugging my friends when we haven't seen one another for a while. In her book, *Hug Therapy*, Kathleen Keaton says that no other form of communication speaks as clearly to another person as physical touch. All of us yearn for meaningful contact with others — by which we can live our potential as balanced adults. The language of touch satisfies our need for spiritual food.

The Touch of Jesus

While He was on earth, Jesus demonstrated God's love by his touch. One day his disciples tried to send away the group of mothers who had brought their children to Him, but He Himself called the children to Him and embraced them. He touched the sick, the blind, the deaf and even lepers spontaneously. And everyone He touched in this way was healed immediately of their ailments or diseases.

It's interesting to note that Jesus singled out those whom the rest of the world usually shunned. We see this clearly when He met the leper. While Jesus walked the earth, lepers were not allowed to live among other people. Nobody dared to touch them because they believed that leprosy was contagious and that they would also become leprous. When the leper therefore met Jesus, he did not expect Jesus to touch him at all – 'Then a leper came to Him, imploring Him, kneeling down to Him and saying to Him, "If You are willing, You can make me clean." And Jesus, moved with compassion, put out His hand and touched him, and said to him, "I am willing; be cleansed." As soon as He had spoken, immediately the leprosy left him, and he was cleansed' (Mark 1:40–42).

Jesus' touch must have been even more wonderful for this man than for others He had healed, because Jesus touched him even before he was healed, that is, while he was still leprous. He probably never forgot the gentle touch of Jesus.

It had probably been years since someone had touched this man. When he was healed after Jesus' touch he told everybody of his miraculous healing, despite Jesus' request not to talk about it. Jesus still wants to spoil his children with his gentle touch. No longer a physical touch, to be sure, but a spiritual touch. However, before He can touch you, you will have to come to Him. You will have to listen carefully to his voice, which we hear in his Word; you will have to consider everything He does for you in depth, and look at everything He has created with amazement ...

However, Jesus not only touches you, He promises that He will bear you and carry you all your life. Find this passage in Isaiah 46:4 and underline it: 'Even to your old age, I am He, and even to gray hairs I will carry you! I have made, and I will bear; even I will carry, and will deliver you.'

Lord Jesus,

I have so often wished to have been alive
when You walked the earth;
that I could have been one of those children
who had been embraced by You,
or a disciple You could have touched.
Thank you that I can still sense your love for me
even though You are no longer on earth.
Thank You that I can see your love in the eyes
of those I love and feel Your love in the hugs
of my family and friends.
Thank you for still touching me –
by your Word and your Spirit and your creation,
and by other people.
Thank you for not only touching me,
but that You also promised to hold me
in the palm of your hand for the rest of my life.
Lord, I also want to touch others and assure them
of my love in the same way.

To say 'I love you'
is merely a combination of
sounds blown away by the wind.
But to touch someone you love
is to write your emotions on his or
her body; they can feel your love.

– Helen Colton

For the love of Christ compels us,
because we judge thus: that if One
died for all, then all died.

– 2 Corinthians 5:14

Are You Drawn or Driven?

'The love of Christ compels us ...' Paul writes in his letter to the church in Corinth. By the word 'compels' he means that it influences us deeply, it encourages us, yes, it draws and invites us to do things.

Stick and Carrot Treatment

Saint Ignatius Loyola, who lived at the beginning of the sixteenth century, is known for his spiritual exercises which helped believers for five centuries to discover and follow God's will for their lives. Ignatius teaches us to distinguish between the work of God and the work of the devil by means of two words, that is, 'drawn' and 'driven'. God draws us to Himself like someone who draws a donkey by holding a carrot to its nose to get it moving. Likewise, God draws his children to do his will. On the other hand, the devil drives people to do the things which are against the will of God, like someone who hurries a donkey by beating it with a stick. These two words are also characteristic of two approaches to religion: The 'stick approach' expects you to acknowledge your sins, your addictions, weaknesses, idols and such things in your life and then do your best to get rid of them. In this way you are therefore supposedly set free from your sin by your own efforts. The 'carrot approach', on the other hand, also requires you to acknowledge your sin and the wrong things in your life, but you are not expected to do this all by yourself. The carrot approach involves focusing your limited energy on the positive things in your life, the things which make you feel you are in touch with God. These things will then take up more and more space in your life and draw you away from the things which are trying to drive you away from God.

In Loyola's 'exercise' he asks you to meditate on your day at the end of every day. Then, in a manner of speaking, you have to separate your clear moments when God was very close to you from the times when God felt far away, and place them in two distinct groups. Ignatius recommended that you then concentrate on the times when you felt closest to God, acted most in harmony with his will, and did the things that made you aware of God's presence in your life.

Seek God's Presence

The next step toward spiritual maturity, says Loyola, is that you do your best to allow these things to play an increasingly important role in your life. If you do this exercise daily you will discover that you will consciously start looking for communication with God and that you will recognise and acknowledge his will in your life. This exercise creates a hunger for God in you; it draws you closer and closer to Him.

However, if you find that you are driven to act in a certain way, you should realise that this is not God working in you. Negative drivenness always comes from the devil. It will be futile to try to do things to escape the consequences of sin (like the Pharisees, in Jesus' time, who tried to burden the Jews with unnecessary man-made laws). Realise that you are helpless and that you yourself cannot put a stop to sinning, but you can rely on Jesus' atoning sacrifice. He has already paid for your sin by taking your sin on Him and paying the full ransom by his death on the cross.

When you look closely at your own life and the things you do, it is not so difficult to know which of these two approaches you are following in your life. Instead of straining against sin, rather make every effort to seek God and to focus on Him.

You will find that this exercise will help you to distinguish more clearly between right and wrong. It will also lead you to new freedom and enable you to serve God of your own free will.

Accept Jesus' invitation in Matthew 11:28–29: 'Come to Me, all you who labor and are heavy laden, and I will give you rest. Take My yoke upon you and learn from Me, for I am gentle and lowly in heart, and you will find rest for your souls.' God wants to draw you to Him today to exchange his light burden for your heavy burden. Do not postpone responding to his call any longer!

Lord,

I'm sorry for so often trying to rid myself
of my many sins by myself.
I now see that it was not only futile
but that I was being driven by a stick!
Thank you for teaching me that You want to draw
me to You with your love for me.
Please help me to distinguish between
the voice of God calling me
and the stick of Satan in my life.
Help me to stop wasting my energy against sin
and to use it to focus on You
and listen to your voice
so I can know and obey your will in my life.
Thank you that this exercise is already enabling
me to live in a new freedom,
to serve and love You of my own free will.

Handling sin correctly starts with ourselves.
When we become aware of things
which prevent us from living
according to the will of God,
we have to confess them to God
and also turn away from them.
Confession of sin changes our lifestyle,
our behaviour, our deeds;
it encourages us to start living
to God's glory time and again.

— Stephan Joubert

And He put all things under His feet, and gave Him to be head over all things to the church, which is His body, the fullness of Him who fills all in all.

– Ephesians 1:22–23

This Is What the Church Should Look Like

A story often conveys a spiritual truth far better than a sermon. In his book *Second Guessing God*, Brian Jones describes a wedding he will never forget.

A Story of a Wedding

Jones says that a complete stranger arrived at their church one day and asked him to perform her wedding ceremony. He actually preferred not to marry complete strangers, but this woman's upperarms were twice the size of his own and she was also at least a head taller than he was, Jones writes tongue in cheek. When he arrived at the house where the ceremony was to be performed, dozens of motorbikes were parked in the driveway. Men with drooping moustaches, leather jackets and helmets were gathered in front of the house, the women looked more like Las Vegas dancing girls than ordinary people, alcohol flowed, and heavy metal music and cigarette smoke were obvious. Just before Jones could take to his heels, one of the strange creatures dragged him into the house. After the intoxicated best man had been leant against the wall, the ceremony began. The bride's massive arms were covered by the lace sleeves of her bridal gown, but the sleeves could not hide the tattoos which covered her arms from shoulder to hand.

The nervous minister tried to run through the ceremony as quickly as possible so he could get home, but the bride insisted on first proposing a toast. 'I want to propose a toast to all of you, because you are like family to me,' she started. She looked at her bridesmaid and said, 'Jackie, you have always been like a sister to me.' The bridesmaid stopped her and said, 'No, you have always been like a sister to me.' With her arms around the bride's neck, she sobbed, 'Do you remember when I lost my baby three years ago? I wouldn't have survived without you.' Then the bride turned to the whole group and confessed, 'I could not have coped without your support. I wanted to die, but you gave me a reason to continue living again.'

With her arm linked through the bridesmaid's the bride continued: 'Richard, when my brother died, you were there for me. You were on a bike tour at the time, but you still visited me every weekend.'

'You were always there for me, too,' one of the men interrupted her. 'When I lost my job, you provided us with groceries and bought our children's school uniforms. I will never forget it. Never.' And so it continued for more than ten minutes. The guests shared their stories: how they had been helped financially when they could not afford a car to get to work; young mothers shared how other women had looked after their children in crisis situations; a man shared how two of the guests had provided him with accommodation when he was released from prison.

Caring little more for Others

Despite his first negative impressions of the wedding guests, Jones realised that day that these people had a tremendous love for one another. When all the stories had been told, the bride lifted her beer glass and said, 'We drink to our friends.'

'I looked around the room,' Jones wrote, 'and realised, this is what the Church should look like.'

This is indeed what the early Christian church looked like. Luke reported that the members of the first Christian church genuinely cared for one another. They shared everything, sold their property and possessions, 'and they distributed to each as anyone had need' (see Acts 4:34–35). The secret of the true church is still that we would care for one another, that we would meet the needs of one another and love one another with the love of Jesus. If your church does not measure up to your expectations, it is time that you once again realise that you are the church, that you form part of the body of Christ. Start with yourself and inspire others to start to truly care for one another.

Lord Jesus,

the church is your Body,
You are the fullness of Him who fills all in all —
and You are also the head of the church.
Thank you that I may form part of your church on earth,
what is more, that I am actually the church.
Forgive me, Lord, that I often complain
about the way my church acts —
because I want things done my way
and lose sight of the fact that
the real characteristic of the church
should be that members love one another,
that they really care for and help one another,
that there is communion of the saints,
that they have one mind and glorify God together.
Thank you for having given each of your children
a gift to use in building your church.
Show me where You want to use me in my congregation.

The church of the Lord,
consisting of many individuals,
nations, peoples and languages,
is one building in which the Spirit of God lives.
The church may therefore not be divided in
itself and be locked in a struggle within itself.
This is a motion of no confidence in our God
and particularly in the redemptive
death of Jesus Christ.

– Johan Smit

For the eyes of the Lʷʲᵃ run to and fro throughout the whole earth, to show Himself strong on behalf of those whose heart is loyal to Him.

– 2 Chronicles 16:9

God Sees You

God is not only omnipotent and omniscient, but also all-seeing. He knows exactly where you are at any given moment and when you need help or want to seek his presence. There is absolutely nothing you can hide from Him. 'And there is no creature hidden from His sight, but all things are naked and open to the eyes of Him to whom we must give account,' says the writer of the letter to the Hebrews (Heb 4:13).

God Does Not See as Man Sees

God does not see as we see. When He asked Samuel to anoint a new king for Israel, Samuel thought the handsome Eliab was the Lord's choice, but the Lord Himself said to him: 'Do not look at his appearance or at his physical [the height of His] stature, because I have refused him. For the LORD does not see as man sees; for man looks at the outward appearance, but the LORD looks at the heart' (1 Sam 16:7).

When Jesus' disciples looked at the man who was born blind, they wondered who was to be blamed for his blindness, he or his parents? The Pharisees were merely concerned because the sabbath was being dishonoured. However, Jesus saw the man himself. Like his Father, He also does not see humankind like we do: Nobody has ever been able to see as 'clearly' as He does. He saw the blind beggar who desperately wanted to touch Him. He noticed Zacchaeus in the tree. He even noticed the woman with the flow of blood although she was in the multitude thronging Him. He noticed the group of children his disciples wanted to send away, and took them in his arms (Mark 10:16).

When Jesus looks at people, it does not end there. His 'looking' always leads to 'action'. He healed the blind man; He invited Himself to stay at Zacchaeus' house; and the woman with the flow of blood was healed as soon as she touched the hem of his garment.

Notice the People Around You

Most of us are inclined not to notice people around us — particularly people who need us. What do you do when a beggar knocks on your door, or when you see someone with a collection box on a street corner? Do you see the many people around you who need your help or who are lonely?

There is a beautiful story of the wealthy American who asked Mother Theresa what emotions she experienced when she walked the streets of Calcutta and saw the numerous people who were terminally ill and dying of hunger. 'I see Jesus in an appalling disguise,' she answered him. Perhaps you are also aware of people who could be Jesus. In fact, He told his disciples, 'Assuredly, I say to you, inasmuch as you did it to one of the least of these My brethren, you did it to Me' (Matt 25:40).

Perhaps it is time that we notice the people around us, like Jesus did, and also do something real to help them, like Jesus did.

John Ortberg wrote a poignant book about God's love for people, *Love Beyond Reason*. He says that we have been placed on earth to do God's work. And what is this work of God? It is simply to see what Jesus would see should He look through my eyes, and to respond as He would have responded. Should all of us do this, we would not only change the circumstances of dozens of other people, but we would also help to solve the situation of poverty in our country, even in the whole world. We ourselves would also change, because you cannot reach out to others in love and still remain the same.

God sees you. Ask Him to enable you to see the world and the people around you through his eyes, and to establish his love in your heart through his Holy Spirit. Then you will find it easy to reach out to them and to help them like Jesus would have done.

Lord Jesus,

thank you for the comforting thought that You see me,
that You know all about me,
that You will never leave me in the lurch,
but that You will always help and assist me;
that I may absolutely rely on You in all circumstances.
Lord, I would like to see people the way You did:
Help me so I will really be able to see people,
to reach out to them and help them,
like You did when You were still on earth.
Let my love no longer merely consist of idle words,
but that my words will give rise to deeds —
and that I will do these things for You
because of your unmerited love for me and
because I would like to give You
something in return out of sheer gratitude.

To be grateful is to recognize the Love
of God in everything He has given us –
and He has given us everything.
Every breath we draw is a gift of his love.

— Thomas Merton

For I am persuaded that neither death nor life, nor angels nor principalities nor powers, nor things present nor things to come, nor height nor depth, nor any other created thing, shall be able to separate us from the love of God which is in Christ Jesus our Lord.

– Romans 8:38

A Matter of Perspective

It's not always easy to see things in the right perspective, to know at all times what really matters. Many people have their priorities quite wrong: We spend most of our time and money on unimportant matters and then omit those which are really important.

There is a funny story of a teenager who wrote a letter to her parents from the school hostel:

Dear Mom and Dad

I have so much to tell you. As a result of the fire in our hostel, which started during student riots, I suffered temporary lung damage and had to be admitted to hospital. While there I fell in love with a sixty-year-old porter and moved in with him. I'm not going to continue my schooling as I'm expecting his child. Unfortunately he lost his job because he drinks too much. We are going to settle in Alaska and perhaps get married there after the baby's birth.

Your daughter

Anna

PS: This is not true at all, but I failed my Math test and I wanted you to see the matter in perspective.

God's Perspective

Catastrophes and misery often hit God's children on earth, causing them to doubt his love. At times everything is strewn with roses and life seems to be a success story from beginning to end. Strangely enough we usually feel very close to God during the bad times – because we then realise that we cannot survive without Him at all. It is nevertheless difficult always to see things in the right perspective and not to land in a pit of despair when things go wrong.

When you know for sure that God still loves you in spite of what is happening to you, and you know He only wants what is best for you, it becomes easier to overcome the discouragement. How you feel about things and how you experience the things happening to you actually depend one hundred percent on your perspective on those things.

'Learning to live in the contentment of being loved means receiving the gift of perspective,' writes John Ortberg. Three of my friends could approach the gruelling chemotherapy for cancer with tremendous positivity and faith because they had the right perspective. They continued to believe that God would bear them up through the suffering – and to date, He has!

Through God's Eyes

As soon as you are able to look at the world and your circumstances through God's eyes of love, your perspective will change so that you will be able to handle everything with God's help. You will discover that God really makes all things work together for the good because He loves you, and that nothing will ever be able to separate you from his love. You will also realise once again that suffering on earth cannot get the better of you because a heavenly glory awaits you.

Paul prays that the love the church members at Philippi have for one another will continue to grow. 'And this I pray, that your love may abound still more and more in knowledge and all discernment, that you may approve the things that are excellent, that you may be sincere and without offense till the day of Christ.' When this happened, Paul promises, they would be able to discern the things which really mattered (see Philippians 1:9–10). Ask God right now to give you the right perspective so that you will be able to discern the things that really matter, and to spend time on them in future.

Heavenly Father,

it's not only wonderfully comforting to know
that nothing can ever separate me from your love,
but it also puts everything into the right perspective for me.
Since I know that You only want what is best for me,
I also believe that You will ultimately
make all things work together for my good.
Please enable me to set my priorities straight
so that I will no longer waste my money and time
on trivial things.
Lord, help me to look at the world
around me through your eyes.
Let my love for You and for others grow.
Help me to develop a better insight
and more sensitivity for others,
so that I will in future be able to discern —
with your help — the things that really matter.
I ask this because I know You love me very much.

You can only succeed in loving others
if you are aware of God's love for you.
When you have discovered that
you are special, and you are experiencing
that God is giving you the strength
to realise this, you can also help others
to achieve their goal in life.
You now also know that
your spiritual power of love
forms the essence of your
meaningful existence on earth.

– Hennie de Villiers

Just as He chose us in Him before the foundation of the world, that we should be holy and without blame before Him in love, having predestined us to adoption as sons by Jesus Christ to Himself, according to the good pleasure of His will.

– Ephesians 1:4–5

God's Choice

There is a beautiful story of a little girl with a harelip who experienced the cruelty of children during her first year at school. They avoided her and made fun of her because she looked different and also spoke with great difficulty. Eventually this little girl believed that nobody would ever love or accept her. In Grade Two she had a new teacher of whom all the children were very fond.

At the school she attended all the children had to do a hearing test every year. For this test every child had to block one ear and repeat out loud a phrase whispered by the teacher. When it was the little girl's turn, she thought the teacher would say something ordinary like: 'The sea is blue.' Or: 'It's hot today.' However, the words the teacher whispered were totally unexpected and changed her whole life. The teacher whispered: 'I wish you were my little girl.'

Everybody feels special when they are chosen by someone else. And usually you are chosen for a specific thing you can do well. When I was at primary school, I knew only too well that I would never be a first choice in games where we had to be able to run fast. Fortunately I fared better when teams were picked for spelling bees or quizzes!

When someone chooses you specially, it means that they would like to have you on their side, that you are noticed and recognised as a unique person with a specific gift.

Unfortunately it also usually means that you are chosen at the expense of someone else. After all, only one captain is needed for the first rugby team and only one class captain is needed at a time.

God Chooses You

God chooses you to be his child, and He made this unlikely choice thousands of years ago – even before He created the world. When God chooses you, it is a choice with a difference – you are not chosen because you are cute or clever or gifted; you are not chosen at the expense of someone else either, because God chooses everyone who wants to be His child. If you belong to Him, it simply means that you have already been chosen by Him. 'But as many as received Him, to them He gave the right to become children of God, even to those who believe in His name,' John wrote in chapter 1:12 of his gospel. However, before God could choose you as his child, Jesus had to be willing to pay the price for your sin on the cross.

If you have not often been chosen by others, know that God chose you specially to belong to Him. You are not only unique and special to Him, but He also equipped you with a special gift by which you can help to make this world a better place. God does not choose you to be idle, but to play a positive role in the world. 'For we are His workmanship, created in Christ Jesus for good works, which

God prepared beforehand that we should walk in them,' Paul writes to the church in Ephesus (Eph 2:10). Don't delay any longer to start doing this!

Heavenly Father,

it absolutely astounds me to know
that You chose me thousands of years ago –
even before the world was created –
that you chose me specially to be your child!
Thank you that I may know that to You I am unique,
that You created me for a specific task,
and equipped me with special talents,
by which I can make the world a better place,
and serve You and other people.
Thank you that this wonderful promise –
that everyone who believes in the Name of Jesus
has the right to be your child – applies to everyone.
Please enable me to identify
and develop my personal gifts and talents
so that I can pursue those good things
which You have specially destined me for
and by which I can glorify your Name.
Lord, I now offer You my specific gifts
willingly and with joy to serve your kingdom.

Each of us has a gift.
Obviously no-one has all the gifts,
but no-one has nothing.
The source is inexhaustible.
That is to say: We do not own the gifts,
they can never belong to us, but they
always remain in the hand of the Spirit.
When we use our gifts freely
and with joy to benefit and bless others,
we serve the healthy functioning
of the body of Christ, yes,
we serve the Lord Himself.

– Johan Cilliers

God so loved the world that He gave His only begotten Son, that whoever believes in Him should not perish but have everlasting life.

— John 3:16

God's Love for People

The great Danish philosopher, Søren Kierkegaard, told a story to demonstrate God's incomprehensible love for humanity:

Once upon a time a young king fell in love with a girl of humble origin. She had no aristocratic connections, no education or status. In fact, she was not even very pretty. She wore tattered clothes and lived in a slum. However, for reasons which no-one could understand, the young king loved this girl so much that he wanted to tell her of his love and ask her to be his wife. He could simply have commanded her to become his queen, of course, because he was an extremely powerful king, but the young ruler knew all too well that power cannot command love. And he desperately wanted her to love him with the same spontaneous passion which he had for her. 'All the power in the world cannot unlock the door to a human heart,' Kierkegaard wrote, 'it must always be opened from the inside.'

The king's councillors advised him to forget about his love for this simple young girl. They suggested that he look for a more suitable bride, but the young king refused. There was only one woman he wanted to marry.

He could obviously have tried to win her heart by giving her expensive gifts, but he realised that should he bring her to his palace to share his pomp and glory, she would be totally overwhelmed. There was only one way in which the young king could show the girl that he truly loved her. He left his throne, removed his crown and took off his royal robe. He put on tattered clothes and moved to a shack to be near the young girl. To win her love he was prepared to change his whole life, to become poor and suffer so she could get to know him at grass roots level.

Jesus Introduces Us to God

This is exactly what God did with us. He sent his only Son, who held the highest position in heaven, to our sinful world to become one of us. Here He was without pomp and glory. His 'road of sorrow' started at his birth in a dirty stable, and ended on a cross where He died for those who wanted to kill Him. He did this so that we would realise exactly how much God loves us, and what He was prepared to sacrifice for us. God is incomprehensibly great and powerful. 'No one has seen God at any time. The only begotten Son, who is in the bosom of the Father, He has declared Him,' John writes in his gospel (John 1:18). If you really want to know how much God loves you, you only have to look at Jesus and realise anew that true love never asks what it can receive, but always what it can give.

And it is God's will that you will love others this way. His unconditional love for you should form the basis of all your relationships in which love plays a role. Ask Him to make your love like His.

Heavenly Father,

the more I meditate on your love for me,
the more I stand amazed
and the more inconceivable and inexplicable
it becomes to me.
Thank you for having done the incomprehensible for me
by demonstrating this love:
You let your Son come into this world,
You let Him experience dreadful suffering,
let Him die on a cross
so my sin could be forgiven
and I could receive eternal life.
You were prepared to sacrifice everything for me,
and You still assure me of your
inconceivable love for me every day
when I read your words in my Bible.
Thank you, Lord!
Please pour your love into my heart by the Holy Spirit
which You have given to me,
so that, in turn, I can pass it on to every person
with whom I come into contact
and so I can love You above all.

God's love is the most
comprehensive, penetrating power in
the universe, and He has poured it out on
us in abundance with the desire that we
should love Him without reserve.
Our love for Him is a mere
fraction of what He desires. Let us
go into the sanctuary of prayer, so the
holy fire of his love can consume us
and we can emanate pure
love more and more.

— Willem Nicol

But when Jesus saw it, He was greatly displeased and said to them, 'Let the little children come to Me, and do not forbid them; for of such is the kingdom of God. Assuredly, I say to you, whoever does not receive the kingdom of God as a little child will by no means enter it.'

– Mark 10:14–15

A Room for Christmas

Adults have often been mortified by the simple, sincere faith of children. Jesus' words that we have to receive his kingdom as little children are only too true — a fact which is clearly illustrated by the following beautiful story.

The big, clumsy Wallace Purling was rather unpopular among his fellow pupils in the small village in the southern part of England where he lived. He was nevertheless always ready to help and defend the younger children. Wally desperately wanted to be a shepherd in the Christmas pageant, but he received the role of innkeeper because his sturdy little body suited the role of the ruthless character.

On the first night of the Christmas pageant the school hall was already packed quite early. Wally watched the huge audience with excitement as he peeked through the chink where the two curtains met. At last the curtains moved back, and Joseph and Mary appeared on the stage. Then Joseph knocked on the wooden door.

'What do you want?' Wally asked, throwing the door open.

'We need somewhere to sleep.'

'Find somewhere else.' Wally said loudly. 'This inn is full.'

'Sir, we have asked all over,' Joseph pleaded again. 'Please, sir, our journey has been long and we are very tired ...'

'There's no room in this inn for you!' Wally's severe face remained inscrutable.

Joseph pleaded again. 'It's my wife, Mary. She's expecting our first child. Is there perhaps somewhere she can rest?'

And then the innkeeper looked down at Mary for the first time. There was a long silence. Long enough for the audience to become uneasy.

'No! Go away!' the prompter whispered from behind the stage curtain.

'No!' Wally echoed obediently. 'Go away!'

Despondently Joseph put his arm around Mary. She leant her head against her husband's shoulder and they walked away slowly. Wally stood in the door, staring at the pathetic little group. His jaw had dropped slightly, a deep frown was on his forehead and bright tears were running down his face.

Suddenly this Christmas pageant became totally different from all the preceding pageants.

'Wait!' the young innkeeper shouted. 'Come back, Joseph! And bring Mary.'

Wally's face was creased with a wide, radiant smile.

'YOU CAN HAVE MY ROOM!'

We Have to Become Like Little Children

Jesus taught his disciples that they have to receive the Kingdom of God like little children, or they would never enter into it. The faith of children is uncomplicated and sincere.

They do not ask proof or answers. Jesus therefore calls them the most important people in his Kingdom. Should you stop questioning everything, or stop bombarding God with your whys and once again believe simply and sincerely like a child, you may know that you have received the Kingdom of God.

Are you prepared to invite God into your life in future with the total surrender of a child? Not merely to set aside some little space in your house for the Christ-child, but to set aside your heart as well?

Lord Jesus,

thank you for your limitless love for me,
thank you that You were prepared to sacrifice heaven
and come into the world as an ordinary human being.
Thank you for having been willing to be born
in an ordinary stable,
to live and work like an ordinary person
and ultimately demonstrate your love on the cross
by dying for me, so the penalty for my sin
could be paid once and for all.
I now offer You my heart and my life.
Give me the faith of a child
who accepts everything with such simplicity
and who is willing to trust You unconditionally.
Thank you for your love and mercy!
Please take full control of my life from today,
so I will no longer belong to myself, but to You.

They are idols of hearts and households;
they are angels of God in disguise;
his sunlight still sleeps in their tresses,
his glory still gleams in their eyes;
those truants from home and heaven
they have made me more manly and mild;
and I know how Jesus could liken
the kingdom of God to a child.

– Charles Dickens

But this I say, brethren, the time is short.

– 1 Corinthians 7:29

When Time Is Running Out

Life Is Linked to Time

Madeleine L'Engele, one of my favourite authors, believes that life has a certain dignity precisely because it is limited. 'Our lives are given a certain dignity by their very evanescence. If there were never to be an end to my quiet moments at the brook, if I could sit on the rock forever, I would not treasure these minutes so much. If our associations with the people we love were to have no termination, we would nog value them as much as we do. Human love is an extraordinary gift, but like all flesh it is corruptible. Death, or distance separates all lovers. My awareness of my husband is sharpened by impermanence. Would we really value anything we could have forever and ever?' she writes.

Redeem Your Time

As we grow older we start realising that our hourglass on earth is running out, and that we should redeem the time we still have left. In an interview with *Die Burger* (30 March 2007), Prof Elise Botha spoke on this subject, saying, 'As you grow older, you realise that you have to consider your time and your strength extremely carefully. However, you are also enormously aware of what still remains to be enjoyed,' she said. 'The tremendous change in your attitude comes incredibly strongly to your attention when you know you now have a factor in your life which you should take into account very, very seriously with regard to time and duration of life.'

When my husband suddenly developed serious angina attacks at the beginning of 2007 and the angiogram brought the bad news that his arteries were so blocked that no treatment would help him, it was an incredible shock. I once again realised that I could not even imagine life without him. I began to appreciate him even more because I did not know how long we would still be together.

While we were relaxing at our beach cottage in Struisbaai the week after the angiogram, we discussed the things we would do if we knew we had only one day left to be together. We also decided that, in future, we would make the very best of our time together and we would build memories together which no-one could ever snatch away from us. Back home we did all the pleasant things we were inclined to postpone because both of us work very hard. We started having coffee together quite often, had a braai even in the middle of the week, went for long drives since walking had become too difficult for him. I did not mind that my husband was not well — as long as I could still have him with me.

Mercifully my husband's health has since improved considerably, and we once again go for long walks without his having an angina attack. However, the illness two years ago has strengthened our relationship and made us more grateful.

The Time You Have Left

Nobody knows how much time we have left on this earth. However, as long as you are alive you have not finished living yet. Share your time with those around you. As long as you can still love, help others, enjoy all the little, trivial, pleasant things in your life, you will still have work on earth. Decide now to make optimal use of the time you have left. Live to the full and with joy, do your work as well as you can. Never allow your time to be merely frittered away and disappear without your being able to show what you have done with it. It has been said that most time is not wasted in hours, but in minutes. Guard your time jealously. Instead of wasting the time at your disposal with things which have no value, start using your time and strength wisely − live your passions, fulfil your dreams, enjoy to the full the things which are fulfilling. Live in such a way that the world will be a better place because you were there. And always remember that the very best time is the time spent with God.

Heavenly Father,

I know all too well that the time is passing
and that I no longer have all the time in the world.
The years are passing ever faster and,
as the time passes, I am gradually discovering
the preciousness of the time I still have left,
that I have to cherish it and use it as well as I can.
I also know I will not always
have the people I love with me
and that we have to start building good memories
which we will still have even when
we are no longer together.
Thank you for the many things we can enjoy together –
that it is your will that your children
enjoy life and rejoice in it.
Help me to live every day to the full,
to set aside enough time for You
and to use to the full every hour I still have left.
Thank you that my time is in your hands,
that You are in my time and that heaven awaits me.

Many people accept time
as time-without-future.
No hope, no prospects, no redemption.
Only routine. Repetition.
Prosperity and adversity
alternating endlessly.
Every day like the day before.
Empty until death.
However, the Christian faith
has the conviction
that God is even there,
that time comes from God,
that God is in time,
and that we have a future with God.
Newness. Surprise. New life. Power.

– Dirkie Smit

You shall also be a crown of glory in the hand of the Lord ... You shall be called Hephzibah ... [The one the Lord loves].

– Isaiah 62:3–4

A God with Hands

Hands have always fascinated me. As a child I often gazed at the strong tanned hands of my father, who was a medical doctor — the hands which could fix everything, help people who had been hurt and hold my small hand tightly when we walked down the street. With my hand in my daddy's hand I had no fear. I also found it wonderful that my mother's small hands were so practical in the kitchen. Our kitchen shelves were always well-stocked with row upon row of bottles filled with jam or canned fruit which she had canned herself — and she also arranged flowers beautifully. The hands of my music teacher also fascinated me — her hands were wrinkled and covered in brown sun spots, yet she could bring forth the most beautiful music from the grand piano in our school hall.

After Matric I studied at the University of Stellenbosch — and there I discovered another aspect of hands. I can still clearly remember the first time the brown-eyed tokkelok (now my husband) took my hand while we were walking down Die Laan. The world suddenly dipped, my knees felt weak (just as it was described in the love stories I used to read), and I never wanted to let go of those strong fingers which held mine. At the birth of our granddaughter I gazed at her hands — the tiny, perfect fingers with the perfectly shaped baby nails folded tightly around her grandmother's thumb even at our first meeting. As she grows older she can twist the men in the family around her little finger with the greatest of ease and her little hands are so quick to learn. Best of all is when she herself picks a flower for Granny or draws happy pictures.

In God's Hand

Some years ago I found the most exceptional woodcarving in a tiny cathedral shop in Germany. A life-sized hand with a tiny figure in the hand had been carved by a master woodcarver. I realised that it was an image of God's hand holding man. Unfortunately it was more than I could afford and fortunately the shop had closed for lunch. I nevertheless often remember the warm feeling of security and protection I experienced when I had looked at it. The woodcarving had conveyed the way God holds me in his hand in an unforgettable way — every day and in every situation.

How wonderful to worship a God who has hands! The gossamer clouds cascading over the deep blue Hottentots-Holland mountain range, a golden-red sunset at the coast, a brown and yellow butterfly on a snow-white rose, the brightly coloured flowers in our small garden, the first bright stars in the evening, the tiniest little insect and every perfect shell, everything is the work of his hands!

God's Handiwork

And this God whose hands fashioned the world so wonderfully beautiful loves me, imperfect as I am! The Bible speaks in various places of the work of God's hands: 'The heavens declare the glory of God; and the firmament shows His handiwork' (Ps 19:1). 'At your right hand are pleasures for evermore' (Ps 16:11). 'Your hands have made me and fashioned me' (Job 10:8). 'For You have formed my inward parts; You have covered me in my mother's womb … for I am fearfully and wonderfully made; marvellous are Your works, and that my soul knows very well' (Ps 139:13–14).

He holds me in such esteem that He made me to have dominion over the works of his hands (Ps 8:6). He has inscribed me on the palms of his hands (Is 49:16). He upholds me with his righteous right hand (Is 41:10) and He therefore assures me that I will never have to be afraid. Even if I walk through the valley of the shadow of death, I will fear no evil (Ps 23:4). His right hand upholds me (Ps 63:8); He has upheld me from birth, He has carried me from the womb: even in my old age. He is, and even to my grey hair He will carry me! He has made me, and will bear me; He will carry, and will deliver me (Is 46:4). Even after death I will be safe in his hands.

Heavenly Father,

how wonderful that I may worship You,
and that our God has hands.
Thank you for your hands which hold me,
carry and guide me throughout my whole life –
from my birth to my old age.
Thank you that my name is engraved
in the palms of your hands,
that I am safe in your hands in times of danger.
Lord Jesus, while You walked the earth
your hands touched and healed people.
I know that no-one can ever snatch me from your hands;
that You were even prepared to die for me on the cross –
that your hands were nailed to the cross –
so my sin could be forgiven and I could be the child of God.
Thank you for also having given me two hands
to reach out to others, hands to help and comfort.
I know that I should be your hands on earth
so You can show your love to others through my hands.

When I look at God,
I seem to see God rolling up his
sleeves and putting his hands
deep into our humanity.
Just look at his hands!
They give and heal,
they cherish everything and
everybody that is precious to Him.
They arrest. Send. Encourage.
And He helps us patiently
to climb the heights.
His hands warn.
Protect. Teach. And lead.
And, when we are most vulnerable,
his hands reach out and save.

– Annalise Wiid

And we know that all things work together
for good to those who love God, to those who
are the called according to His purpose.

– Romans 8:28

Everything Works Together for Good

Romans 8:28 has always been one of the most comforting verses in the Bible to me. If you have it as your motto, nothing can really go wrong in your life. God uses everything that happens in your life — bad as well as good — to realise his purpose in your life, and if you love God, you know for a fact that everything will eventually work together for your good. After all, your life is in God's hands, He is fully in control of your future and ultimately all things will work together for his glory — and for you.

John Baillie wrote a striking prayer on this:

> Teach me. O God, to use all the circumstances of my life today that they may bring forth in me the fruits of holiness rather than the fruits of sin.
> Let me use disappointment as material for patience:
> Let me use success as material for thankfulness:
> Let me use suspence as material for perseverance:
> Let me use danger as material for courage:
> Let me use reproach as material for longsuffering:
> Let me use praise as material for humility:
> Let me use pleasures as material for temperance:
> Let me use pains as material for endurance.

God can use anything that happens to you positively. It is possible for Him to teach you patience by permitting disappointments in your life; to make you successful to teach you the meaning of gratitude, to allow problems in your life to teach you perseverance, to expose you to danger to teach you courage, and to test your endurance by allowing you to suffer.

Suffering Has a Plus

Even the suffering which God permits in your life ultimately has so many pluses that it should be a reason for joy.

In James 1:2 and Romans 5:3 these reasons are spelled out for us: You may rejoice in suffering, writes James, because the suffering in your life causes a chain reaction: If your faith endures the test, it produces perseverance, and perseverance produces spiritual maturity in your life. In Paul's letter to the Romans, he agrees with James: Suffering in our lives produces perseverance, he says. This perseverance in turn produces sincerity of faith, and sincerity of faith produces hope, and hope in God never fails, because God has poured out His love in our hearts by the Holy Spirit Who was given to us (see Romans 5:3–5).

Regardless of what happens to us, you may always be assured of God's presence, and that He will never withdraw his grace from you. His purpose with suffering is to strengthen your faith so you can learn to endure. You never have to give up your hope either — your hope that you will one day share God's glory — because you know God will never disappoint the hope of his children. 'A feature of Biblical hope is an absolute assurance and a keen expectation. There is no room for doubt and uncertainty,' the *Bybellennium* says about this verse. Hold on to this hope when you experience a period of suffering — and ask God to help you to rejoice in it!

Heavenly Father,

it is good to know that my life is totally in your hands
and that You are fully in control.
Thank you that I may know
that You will ultimately allow all things
— even the most negative things —
to work together for my good and your glory.
I can now see that even the times of suffering in my life
have so many pluses that I may be grateful for them,
because suffering teaches me
to believe in You even more deeply,
faith teaches me to persevere,
and perseverance ultimately leads to spiritual maturity.
Thank you that my hope in You will never be disappointed,
because You Yourself poured out your love into my heart
by the Holy Spirit whom You gave to me.
Please help me to handle everything that happens in my life
— even the things I would rather have had differently —
in such a way that it will bring forth
the fruit of holiness in my life.

You Have No Choice!
Either you bear your cross,
or the cross will break you.
However, you can only bear the cross
once you have learnt to understand its
meaning and function.
The cross cannot save you from
suffering, but it will save you from the
senselessness and futility of it.
— Phil Bosmans

These all died in faith, not having received
the promises, but having seen them afar off
were assured of them, embraced them and
confessed that they were strangers
and pilgrims on the earth.

– Hebrews 11:13

Unanswered Prayers

Philip Yancey made a study of the prayers of Christians who were persecuted and to his amazement discovered that they had not asked to be saved from their circumstances, but asked for strength to endure the circumstances; they prayed for strength and courage in the midst of suffering. Yancey also studied the prayers of the early martyrs, and they had prayed for their families they had to leave behind, for more faith, for the courage to approach death fearlessly. Some even thanked God for the privilege to suffer for Him, and others asked forgiveness for their persecutors.

We often read in the Bible of prayers that God apparently did not answer. The best known of these unanswered prayers is probably Jesus' prayer in Gethsemane. The prayerful songs of praise of Zacharias and Mary in Luke 1 also ended in totally different ways from what we would have expected: Mary stands at the foot of a cross and sees her Son suffering and dying — and Zacharias' son was decapitated by the very enemies from whom Jesus had to save his people. In Hebrews 11:13 we read about a group of people who also had not received what they had been promised: 'These all died in faith, not having received the promises, but having seen them afar off were assured of them, embraced them and confessed that they were strangers and pilgrims on the earth.' Their unanswered prayers had made them realise that they were merely 'strangers and pilgrims' on the earth, and that their real fatherland was in heaven. We simply do not know why God answers the prayers of some of his children while the prayers of others remain unanswered.

The Story of a Cemetery

In Yancy's book *Prayer* he tells the moving story of the cemetery in Miango, Nigeria. Prof Charles Edward White of Michigan taught at the University of Jos in Nigeria for a while. While he was there, he visited the missionaries' cemetary on the central plateau in Nigeria. He noted that the majority of the graves were the graves of young children. Thirty-three of the sixty-five graves were those of young children. Two of the babies had lived only one day. Others lived a few years before they also succumbed to tropical diseases. Prof White thought a long time about the pain these deaths must have caused the missionaries. The missionaries went to Nigeria of their own free will and were aware of the dangers, but their children had no choice in the matter. 'The cemetary in Miango tells us something about God and his grace,' Prof White wrote after his visit. 'It shows us that God is not the kind grandfather who fulfils all our wishes. The parents obviously would have wanted their children to survive. They probably pleaded with God to heal them, but He did not answer their prayers. The cemetary also teaches us that although God's grace is given freely, it is definitely not cheap grace. The only way to understand the story told by the cemetary in Miango, is to remember that God also buried his Son on the mission field.'

God Knows Best

'If you want to see God smile, you have to tell Him about your plans,' the old saying goes. God always knows best. He probably often smiles when we ask for things He knows will not be good for us. This is why some of our prayers remain unanswered.

Sometimes we are baffled as to why our prayers remain unanswered while we believe them to be in line with God's will, such as the deaths of the many missionary children buried in Miango. When you pray and your prayer remains unanswered, you may rest assured that God knows what is best for you, and that his answer to your prayers is best for you. We know this from the verse we discussed in our previous daily reading: 'And we know that all things work together for good to those who love God, to those who are called according to His purpose' (Rom 8:28).

Heavenly Father,

please forgive me for so often having been upset
when You did not answer my prayers
according to my will.
Forgive me for so often having asked things from You
which were selfish and self-centred ...
I now realise that You have probably often smiled
about my silly requests ...
Thank you that I may still pray
and come boldly to your throne of grace
with the sure knowledge that your response to my prayers
will always be the very best for me
even when You do not always fulfil all my wishes.
Thank you for being omniscient,
that your grace for me is so infinitely great.
Lord, teach me once again to pray like Jesus in Gethsemane;
to submit my will to your will
and to trust You to answer my prayer requests
so that all things will work together for my good
because You know what is best for me.

Prayer is not a matter of getting
what we want the most.
Prayer is a matter of giving ourselves
to God and learning his laws,
so that He can do through us
what He wants the most.

— Agnes Sanford

But you are a chosen generation, a royal priesthood, a holy nation, His own special people, that you may proclaim the praises of Him who called you out of darkness into His marvelous light.

—1 Peter 2:9

Why Are You Here?

Questions Without Answers

Douglas Adams wrote a fantasy story entitled *The Hitchhiker's Guide to the Galaxy*. A computer called Deep Thought features in this story. Deep Thought is supposed to be able to answer all questions. Two scientists wanted to know the answer to life, the universe and everything from Deep Thought. The computer answered by asking them to return in 7,5 million years as it would then have the answer ready. After the 7,5 million years had passed, another group of scientists gathered around the computer. They were accompanied by a vast crowd of people who were also keen to hear the computer's answer. 'What is the answer to life, the universe and everything?' the scientists asked again. 'Forty-two,' the computer answered. Definitely not a satisfactory answer!

All of us are looking for an answer to the question as to exactly why we were placed on earth. To find these answers we usually make use of our own intellect. But like the computer's answer, our own answers will never be satisfactory. We should rather turn to God, to God's Word, for the answer, because if we omit Him from our thinking processes and our search for answers to vital questions, we will never find the right answer.

You Were Created to Honour God

In his bestseller, *Purpose-Driven Life,* Rick Warren tries to answer these questions.

God made everything for his glory, he says. And your greatest achievement in life is to live to his glory. You do this by worshipping Him, by loving others, by becoming more like Jesus, by serving others with your gifts, and telling others about Him.

You were planned for God's pleasure. Everything you do to please Him is worship — worship should therefore not only form part of your life, but it should encompass your whole life. God wants to have a relationship with you, and He smiles when you love, trust, obey Him; when you praise and thank Him and use your abilities.

You were formed for God's family. He becomes part of your life when you talk to Him in prayer, think about Him and spend time with Him. Your whole life should revolve around this love. Spending time with God is the best expression of this love and now is the best time to love.

You created to become like Christ. God's Spirit works in you to make you more like Jesus by making you faithful to the guidelines in his Word, and to encourage you to do what the Bible teaches you. He uses problems and temptations in your life to make you grow spiritually.

You were shaped for serving God. You have been created to dedicate your life to do the good deeds God has specially created you for. God has given each of his children special gifts by which we can glorify Him and serve others. Discover your own gifts and use them to turn this world into a better place.

Finally, you have been made for a misson, so other people can come to know Jesus by your testimony. Only then do you really fulfil God's purpose on earth.

Look carefully at Warren's six reasons why God has placed you on earth, and make time every day to pursue them.

Heavenly Father,

thank you for the six clear answers
as to why You have placed me on earth.
I now realise that You have made me for your glory
and to glorify You with my whole life;
that I have been made specially to make You smile
by loving You, trusting, praising and thanking You,
and by being in a love relationship with You.
I am privileged to form part of your family,
and to talk to You and spend time with You.
Please make me more like Jesus
by helping me to do the things
You ask me to in your Word.
I want to set aside more time for You,
and dedicate my life to the good works
You have made me for,
by using my gifts to glorify You and to serve others.
Please send me out to proclaim your good news
so others will learn to know and love You
through my example.

The purpose of your life is far greater
than your own personal fulfilment, your
peace of mind, or even your happiness.
It's far greater than your family, your career, or
even your wildest dreams and ambitions.
If you want to know why you were placed on
this planet, you must begin with God ... You
were made by God and for God – and until
you understand that, life will never make sense.
It is only in God that we discover our origin,
our identity, our meaning, our purpose,
our significance and our destiny.
Every other path leads to a dead end.

–Rick Warren

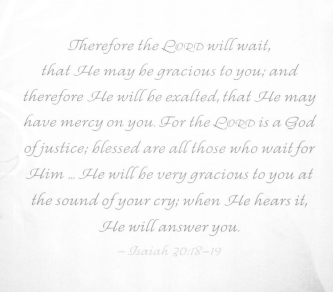

Therefore the LORD will wait,
that He may be gracious to you; and
therefore He will be exalted, that He may
have mercy on you. For the LORD is a God
of justice; blessed are all those who wait for
Him ... He will be very gracious to you at
the sound of your cry; when He hears it,
He will answer you.

– Isaiah 30:18–19

The Wonder of Answered Prayer

The Power of Prayer

When God's children call to Him, miracles happen. Should we really understand the power which is released when we pray, we would spend half the day on our knees, writes Terry Meeuwsen. Hudson Taylor alleges that the power of prayer has never been utilised fully. If we want to see the powerful work of God's power and grace, we have to respond to God's standing invitation in Jeremiah 33:3 by calling to Him: 'Call to Me,' He invites us, and continues, 'and I will answer you, and show you great and mighty things, which you do not know.'

Some time ago a friend sent us an e-mail with an incredible story of answered prayer. A young mother had died at a mission station and the staff were left with a sobbing two-year-old girl and a premature baby that had to be kept warm in some way or other. The only hot-water bottle to stabilise the baby's body temperature was leaking as a result of age and there was no way whatsoever of finding another hot-water bottle in that distant place. When the children in the orphanage heard of this problem, a little girl called Ruth prayed as follows with the honest sincerity of a child: 'Lord, please send us a hot-water bottle today. Tomorrow will be too late because the baby will then be dead. Please send it this afternoon.' While the doctor was still gasping at this presumptuous prayer, the little girl added; 'And since You are sending the hot-water bottle, please put a doll in the parcel as well — for the little girl who is crying because her mummy has died, so that she will know You love her ...'

The doctor knew that God could do anything, but the only way this prayer could be answered in their circumstances would be a parcel sent from home, and during the preceding four years she had never received anything like this. And in any case, who on earth would place a hot-water bottle and a doll in a parcel addressed to a mission station on the equator! Halfway through the afternoon a parcel was delivered to the doctor's house. She immediately called the orphans to help her open the parcel. Carefully, reverently, the string was untied knot by knot, and the layers of paper were removed one by one. About thirty pairs of eyes watched expectantly as the contents were taken from the parcel. At the top was beautiful, multicoloured clothing for the little ones and the doctor immediately started handing it out. Then there were bandages for the leprous patients, mixed dried fruit for vitamins — and when the doctor put her hand into the box again she felt it ... No, this was impossible! However, when she removed it, it was unmistakably a brand new hot-water bottle. The doctor was in tears. Ruth was standing at the head of the group of children. She immediately called out: 'If the Lord has sent the hot-water bottle He would certainly have included the doll for the little girl.'

Without waiting she started scrabbling in the box herself and, yes, she took out a doll! 'May I give it to the little girl so that she can know God loves her?' she requested spontaneously.

This parcel had been on its way from the mission doctor's hometown for five months. It had been packed by a Sunday School class where the Sunday School leader had heeded the voice of the Lord on an impulse — down to the hot-water bottle and a doll! And the parcel had been wrapped five months before a little girl in Africa had prayed that the Lord should send the hot-water bottle that very day.

When God Says No

Every child of God has probably already discovered that God does not answer every prayer in such a spectacular way. Sometimes we ask for things that are not according to the will of God; sometimes our prayers are selfish to fulfil our own dreams; sometimes we do not receive what we ask for because God has something even better in mind for us. God sees further than we do, and just as you would not give your baby a toy that could hurt him, God will not answer prayers that could have negative consequences in your life.

God knows exactly what you need. Trust Him to give you the right answer to your prayers. Remember this, particularly when the answer to your prayer differs from the answer you wanted so desperately.

Heavenly Father,

You are so incredibly wonderful!
You know all my needs and
sometimes answer my prayers even before I call;
You fulfil my prayers even
before I make them known to You.
I know You love me and listen to my prayers,
although I am only an insignificant sinful being
and You are the great God Who created the universe.
Please teach me to pray
with the absolute confidence of a child,
so that I will simply submit my needs to You
with the certainty that You can do everything –
even that which seems humanly impossible to me.
Teach me also to be satisfied
with your answers to my prayers
even when they sometimes differ
from the answer I was hoping for.
I praise You because your Word says
that You are eager to be gracious to me.

Prayer covers the whole of a man's life.
There is no thought, feeling, yearning or
desire, however low, trifling, or vulgar we may
deem it, which, if it affects our real interest or
happiness, we may not lay before God and
be sure of his sympathy. His nature is such
that our often coming does not tire Him.
The whole burden of the whole life of every
man may be rolled on to God and not weary
Him, though it has wearied the man.

— Henry Ward Beecher

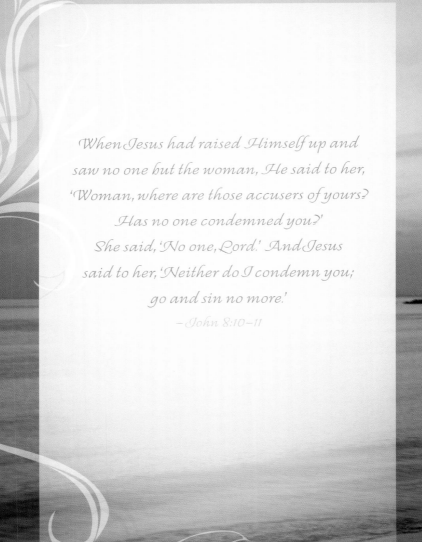

When Jesus had raised Himself up and
saw no one but the woman, He said to her,
'Woman, where are those accusers of yours?
Has no one condemned you?'
She said, 'No one, Lord.' And Jesus
said to her, 'Neither do I condemn you;
go and sin no more.'
– John 8:10–11

A Second Chance

Jesus was always prepared to give people another chance. To the woman caught in adultery He said that He did not judge her, but that He expected her to stop sinning.

This reminds me of the story of a man called Alfred who had the strange experience of reading his own obituary. Owing to a misunderstanding on the editorial staff of the local newspaper of his hometown, his obituary was published while he was still as fit as a fiddle. Alfred Nobel had made a fortune through his discovery of dynamite in 1867. Although he was generous toward everybody, his obituary blamed the discovery of dynamite for the deaths of thousands of people.

The news report called him a 'pedlar of death'. Alfred was justly shocked about this opinion regarding his life's work, and he immediately decided that this was not the way he wanted to be remembered. Consequently we no longer associate the name Alfred Nobel with dynamite but with peace, knowledge and scientific progress. People like Mother Theresa, Martin Luther King, Theodore Roosevelt and the South Africans Albert Luthuli, Nelson Mandela and FW de Klerk have received this prize. Alfred Nobel grasped the second chance he received with both hands. When he died eight years later, he was highly praised by everyone. His 'second' obituary was also totally different from the first one.

Change Your Life

It's never too late to change your own life and become the person God wants you to be. In his book *Embracing Soul Care,* Stephen W Smith says that many criteria of true success are never acknowledged by modern society:

- I am successful if I lead a fulfilled life, not if my life is filled with possessions.
- I am successful if my life has meaning and direction; if I have a meaningful reason for rising every day and tackling my day.
- I am successful if I reveal character and integrity.
- I am successful if my own story fits in with the story God has written for me.
- I am successful if I am surrounded by people who, like me, are trying to obey the Biblical guidelines.
- I am successful if I finish my race on earth successfully.
- I am successful if it is my goal to love God and others sincerely for the next twenty-four hours.
- I am successful if I walk humbly before God.
- I am successful if I do not need others to endorse my success.
- I am successful if one day, when I reach heaven, God will say to me, 'Well done!'

What Is Your Legacy?

Everyone of us leaves a legacy on earth.

The legacies of many (ordinary) people are invisible, while the legacies of other (famous) people are extremely visible. We all know about the exceptional things people like Anton Rupert and Nelson Mandela did in our country and what they leave as material and moral legacies. The legacies of others, like your mom or your aunt whom nobody but your family knew well, are known only to those who were close to them. For example, our congregation supports two young women who care for more than one dozen Aids orphans — and very few people are aware of the incredible contribution of these women. Another woman manages a workshop for handicapped persons without any remuneration, and two of our friends are involved in a literacy programme for schools in Mozambique. Their names will never appear in the headlines of newspapers, yet they do far more in God's kingdom than many wealthy, famous and well-known people, and theirs are the legacies which actually have God's blessing.

After Neil Armstrong had left the first footprints on the moon, NASA reported that his footprints would remain undisturbed in the moon dust for ten million years because there is no atmosphere, wind or weather on the moon that could wipe the footprints away. I can still remember this impressive event clearly because, although we still had no television in South Africa at that stage, I was privileged to observe the event. My husband was a lecturer at the University of the Orange Free State at the time and they had a special broadcast of the moon landing at the university.

During our life on earth, we all leave our individual footprints. What do yours look like? What legacy will you leave your children? How will your obituary read? As Alfred Nobel discovered, it is never too late for a second chance — not for you either. You still have time to change your life for the better, to make it more meaningful by realising God's dreams for you and realising his purpose for your life.

Lord Jesus,

when You were on earth You gave
so many people second chances
by healing them and changing their lives.
Thank you for offering me another chance as well:
Thank you that it's not yet too late
to change my life for the better.
I want to live according to your criteria
of success from today:
I want to live a fulfilled life so that my life
will have meaning and direction.
I want to reveal character and integrity,
obey the guidelines in your Word,
complete my race successfully,
love You and others sincerely;
I want to be humble and pursue your approval
rather than the approval of others.
I want to leave a spiritual legacy
of which my children and friends will be proud.
Lord, please enable me to do this.

Change has a considerable
psychological impact on the human mind.
To the fearful it is threatening because
it means that things may get worse.
To the hopeful it is encouraging because
things may get better. To the confident
it is inspiring because the challenge
exists to make things better.
– King Whitney Jr

Does not wisdom cry out, and understanding lift up her voice? ... Counsel is mine, and sound wisdom; I am understanding, I have strength. By me kings reign, and rulers decree justice.

— Proverbs 8:1, 14–15

Ten Guidelines for Success

A Great Secret

One of the things I enjoy most is to come across a table with secondhand books and to browse around looking for gems. My husband is not too impressed by this way of spending my time! One of the gems I found at such a book table for just a few cents was Og Mandino's *The Greatest Secret in the World.* My copy is rather tattered, some of the pages stick together and can hardly be separated; but this battered little book contains many precious thoughts. The *Ten Great Scrolls of Success* are also recorded in this little book, and I would like to share these ten guidelines with you:

1. Today I begin a new life.
2. I will greet this day with love in my heart.
3. I will persist until I succeed.
4. I am nature's greatest miracle.
5. I will live this day as if it is my last.
6. Today I will be master of my emotions.
7. I will laugh at the world (Keep perspective).
8. Today I will multiply my value a hundredfold.
9. I will act now, I will act now, I will act now.
10. I will pray for guidance.

Mandino assures his readers that if they would read each of these ten guidelines carefully every day for a period of thirty days, their lives would change for the better, and their failures of the past would be turned into successes. In due course the contents would become so much part of their lives that they would instinctively conform to them. How about it — don't you feel like trying to do this exercise? I will give you a brief summary of how Mandino explains each guideline.

1. Today I Begin a New Life

I undertake to cultivate only good habits from today and to follow them slavishly, so that they can replace my bad habits of the past. I will wake up every morning with new energy, more than I have ever experienced before. My energy will increase, my enthusiasm will grow and my desire to embrace the world will become stronger so that I will be happier than I thought possible in this world of strife and unhappiness.

2. I Will Greet This Day With Love in My Heart

This is the greatest secret of success, because only love can open the hearts of people. I will praise my enemies so they can become friends; I will encourage my friends so they will become my brothers. I will greet everyone I meet in a silent greeting with the words: 'I love you'. Although they will not be able to hear the words, they will be able to see it in my eyes, recognise it in my smile, and hear the echo in my voice. It will unlock their heart. I will also love myself, because when I do, I will examine everything that enters my body, my mind, my spirit and my heart carefully. From today I will let go of all hatred, because I no longer have time to hate, only time to love. I will approach this day with love in my heart, therefore I will be successful.

3. I Will Persist Until I Succeed

The rewards of life are usually handed out at the end of the journey, and nobody knows how many steps will still be required to reach the goal. I may still experience failure even when I give my thousandth step, and nevertheless meet success just around the next turning. I will therefore still continue to take another step.

I will never consider failure as a possibility and will remove phrases such as 'lose courage', 'can't', 'impossible', 'fail' and 'hopeless' from my vocabulary. I will try to avoid despair, but should I become desperate, I will continue in spite of it. I will ignore the obstacles at my feet and keep my eyes on the goals ahead. I will greet every day with the confidence that today will be the very best day of my life. As long as I have my breath, I will persevere, because if I continue, I will succeed.

4. I Am Nature's Greatest Wonder

There has never before been anyone else with exactly my brain, my heart, my eyes, my ears, my hands, my hair and my mouth. Nobody has ever spoken, thought or moved like me. I am a unique being. I am no longer going to try to copy others, but enjoy my uniqueness. I will bear in mind that my gifts, my mind, my heart and my body will stagnate and die unless I use them well.

I have been placed on earth for a specific purpose. I have at last discovered that all my problems, disappointments and grief are actually great opportunities.

5. I Will Live This Day As If It Is My Last

I will not waste a single minute on the failure and grief of yesterday, because yesterday is forever past and I will no longer think about it. I will cherish every hour of today, because I will never have it again.

I will complete today's tasks. I will cuddle my children while they are still young and love my spouse while he/she is still with me. I will help a friend in need and give all I can. I will work as hard as I can. If today is my last day, I will make it my greatest monument. Today I will live every minute to the full, make every hour count. I will live as if today were my last day, and if it's not, I will kneel down to say thank you.

6. Today I Will Be Master of My Emotions

If my attitude is wrong, my day will be a disaster. People who allow their thoughts to control their actions are weaklings, but those who compel their actions to control their thoughts are strong. I will follow this plan of action every day:

- When I feel depressed, I will sing;
- When I feel sad, I will laugh;
- When I feel ill, I will work even harder;
- When I am scared, I will go forward;
- When I feel inferior, I will put on new clothes;
- When I am uncertain, I will speak louder;
- When I experience poverty, I will think of the wealth awaiting me;
- When I feel incompetent, I will remember my successes of the past;
- When I feel small, I will remember my objectives.

7. I Will Laugh at the World (Keep Perspective)

Of all God's creatures only humans can laugh. I have received the gift of cheerfulness and I can use it whenever I like. I will therefore try to laugh more. I will smile and improve my digestion, I will laugh and my burdens will become lighter; I will roar with laughter and live longer.

I will also laugh at myself, because humans are at their most comical when they take themselves too seriously. I will enjoy today's happiness today; it cannot be saved for tomorrow. I will laugh at my failures and they will disappear in the clouds of new dreams; I will laugh at my successes and they will shrink to their true value. I will laugh at the goodness of people and multiply it. As long as I can laugh I will never be poor. Only with cheerfulness and happiness can I really be a success and enjoy the fruit of my labour.

8. Today I Will Multiply My Value a Hundredfold

When you want corn to grow and increase, you have to plant the grains in the dark soil. My failures, my hopelessness and my shortcomings are the darkness in which I am 'planted' so that I can grow. I have the power to make my dreams come true and to choose my calling. I will set my objectives for my day, my week, my month, my year and for my life. While I pursue this objective I will remember my best achievements in the past and improve them a hundredfold. This will be the standard against which I will measure myself in the future. When I stumble, I will get up; only a worm cannot stumble because he is already so close to the ground, and I am not a worm. I will never aim low or remain satisfied with my previous achievements. I will always set myself higher objectives as soon as I have achieved the previous ones. I will always strive to make the next hour better than the present one.

9. I Will Act Now, I Will Act Now, I Will Act Now

I will act now. I will not try to avoid today's tasks, because I do not know whether tomorrow will ever dawn. I will act now — with these words I will approach every challenge the future may hold for me. I will act now, because now is the only time of which I can be sure. Tomorrow is the day for the work of the lazy. And I'm not lazy. Success waits for no one. If I postpone, I can lose my beloved for ever. Now is the time. This is the place. I am the one. I will act now.

10. I Will Pray for Guidance

Who has so little faith that he does not call to God in moments of catastrophe or grief? Who has not yet prayed when they are confronted with danger, death or incomprehensibilities? All people instinctively ask for help. And is this call for help not a kind of prayer?

From today I will pray, but my prayers will only be a request for guidance. I will never ask for material things. Not for gold, love, good health, triumph, renown, success or happiness. I will only pray for God's guidance. The guidance that I pray for may come, or perhaps it cannot be realised. However, aren't both of these possibilities already an answer?

Creator of all things, help me.

For this day I go out into the world naked and alone,
and without your hand to guide me I will wander far from
the path which leads me to success and happiness ...
I ask not for gold or garments or even opportunities equal
to my ability; instead, guide me so that I may acquire
ability equal to my opportunities ...
Help me to remain humble through obstacles and failures;
yet hide not from mine eyes the prize
that will come with victory.
Assign me tasks to which others have failed;
yet guide me to pluck the seeds
of success from their failures.
Confront me with fears that will temper my spirit;
yet endow me with courage to laugh at my misgivings.
Spare me sufficient days to reach my goals;
yet help me live this day as if it were my last.
Bathe me in good habits that the bad ones may drown;
yet grant me compassion for the weaknesses in others.
Suffer me to know that all things shall pass;
yet help me to count my blessings of today.
Expose me to hate so it be not a stranger ...
yet fill my cup with love to turn strangers into friends.
Let me become all you planned for me ...

(from 'Prayer of a salesman' in *The Greatest Secret in the World*.)

*Everyone who complies with
the provisions of success will,
from time to time, receive the proof
that he has succeeded as a person
because, deep down, this is
success after all.*

—Johan Heyns

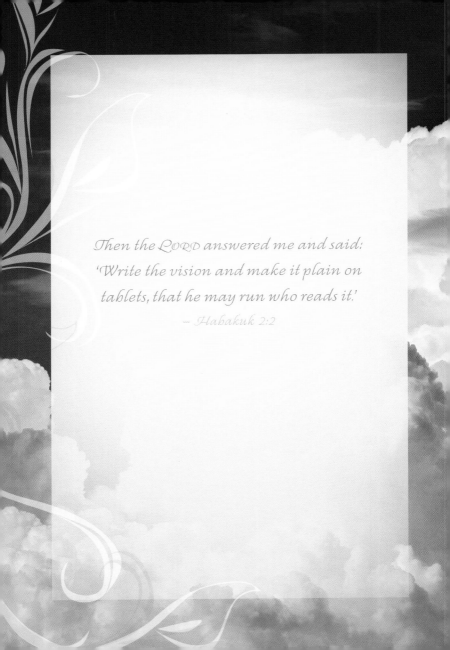

Then the LORD answered me and said:
'Write the vision and make it plain on
tablets, that he may run who reads it.'
– Habakuk 2:2

Give Me My Books!

The Joy of Books

I have been crazy about books from a tender age. If fire should ever break out in our house, my books would probably be the first things I would save! I spent so much time in our town library in my primary school years that I had eventually worked through all the children's books. In an effort to keep me away from the 'adult literature', the librarian taught me to help her in the library. I also helped to select the 'new children's books' every few months when the 'book truck' arrived in our town. Books have always been one of the greatest joys in my life. I can still remember when I discovered Kahlil Gibran's book, *Sand and Foam,* in the library. (I think I was in Grade Five at the time.) On account of the nude drawings I could not risk taking the book home with me, but the words sang to me — I just had to have them where I could read them again and again. I therefore sat down and copied the whole book into an old exercise book! The librarian probably thought I was working on a school project.

It was therefore not difficult to choose a course at Stellenbosch — a Diploma in Librarianship was my first choice. After my studies my work as a librarian was a daily joy, and when I was appointed as book selector, my cup practically ran over. One of my dreams was to be able to write a book myself. And at the moment being able to write is just as satisfying as reading. I can really say that my 'work' is a daily joy, even though I will never be able to play in the Tolstoy or Dostoyevski league.

The Support of Books

'When I feel depressed nothing can help me as much as my books. They are the best sustenance I have ever found for this journey of life. And I really pity people who do not know the joy and support books offer,' Michel de Montaigne quite rightly says.

'I was an extremely happy child,' Riana Scheepers writes in her book, *'n Engel in my huis.* 'Not because my parents were famous and wealthy and flamboyant. On the contrary, we were an unimportant family in an unimportant village in a rural area. Yet even as a child I was famous and wealthy and flamboyant and I had the opportunity to travel all over the world. And not only the world, but also through the centuries ... I was a very wealthy and privileged child because I was always surrounded by books and stories.'

When we recently had to move to a smaller house in a security complex, I had to get rid of some of my beloved books. I therefore checked my bookshelves conscientiously and put all the books I had not read for a long time and those which were not absolute favourites in cardboard boxes — only to place them back on the shelves after a while! My books are my friends — I cannot survive without any of them.

Spiritual Books

Of all my many books, my spiritual books are the ones that mean the most to me. 'Without books God is silent,' Thomas Bartolin quite rightly says. Spiritual books are vital if you want to grow spiritually. They can change your thinking, your opinions and even your life. The very best thing you can do for yourself is to collect a personal library of spiritual books. You cannot go wrong with authors such as Philip Yancey, Joni Eareckson-Tada, John Ortberg and CS Lewis. To recognise a kindred spirit in an author for the first time is a spiritual delight. I recently got hold of a book by Steven James for the first time — and what a joy!

The Most Wonderful Book

The Bible is still the most incredible book of all books ever written. It is a lasting inspiration to me and the most important source from which all my own books flow. When you study statistics about the Bible, you cannot fail to discover afresh the wonder and uniqueness of the Bible. It was written over a period of more than three thousand years by more than forty authors in three languages and on three continents ... yet it forms a perfect unity with the same basic message: God loves you so much that He sent his Son to the earth to pay for your sin so that you can become his child. The Bible is the only book that has been translated into most of the existing languages, and has headed the best-seller list for more than one hundred years.

Never take the Bible for granted. Make time to study your Bible in depth and memorise as many verses from it as possible. This way you will always and every day have your Bible with you. In this way, God will speak to you personally every day, and you will get to know Him better and learn to love Him more day by day.

Heavenly Father,

today I want to thank you for the sheer joy
and support of books.
Thank you for the thousands of books which I have
been able to read in the course of my own life;
for the joy and inspiration and wisdom
which they have keyed into my life.
You speak to me every day through my books —
particularly through your Word, the Bible.
I take the message of that Word with me every day,
it reminds me of your incredible love for me day by day.
Teach me to set aside more time to listen
to your voice in your Word,
so that it will indeed be a light to my path
and a lamp to my feet.

Books are readily available,
and what companions they are.
A good book is the same today as yesterday.
It is never displeased when we put it down;
it is always inspiring when we pick it up.
It never fails us in times of adversity.

– Fulton J Sheen

But we all, with unveiled face, beholding as
in a mirror the glory of the Lord, are being
transformed into the same image from glory
to glory, just as by the Spirit of the Lord.

– 2 Corinthians 3:18

Metamorphosis

When I was growing up and still at primary school, I also had silkworms like most little girls. I was totally fascinated by the changes they underwent: The gruesome white larvae spun a golden silk cocoon around themselves, and then the cocoons turned into the hard brown chrysalises, which were left after we had pulled off the silk thread. These chrysalises then turned into white moths! This was much more than a mere change — it was a total metamorphosis!

Change Is God's Will

God wants his children to undergo just such a total metamorphosis. It is his will that we, who are unholy sinners, should become holy children of God — yes, mirrors of his glory. Such a radical change sounds as impossible as a larva which first becomes a chrysalis and then a moth. It does not involve a small adjustment, but a radical change. Just as I could hardly believe that a larva could turn into a moth, nobody should ever be able to recognise the old sinful creatures we used to be in the new creatures God wants to turn us into.

'God became man to turn creatures into sons: not simply to produce better men of the old kind but to produce a new kind of man', CS Lewis writes. 'It is not like teaching a horse to jump better and better but like turning a horse into a winged creature. Of course, once it has got its wings, it will soar over fences which it could never have been jumped ...'

What is more, God wants you to become like Jesus – and 'Christ is the image of God' (2 Cor 4:4). 'For whom He foreknew, He also predestined to be conformed to the image of His Son, that He might be the firstborn among many brethren,' Paul writes to the church in Rome (Rom 8:29). And he encourages the believers in Ephesus: 'Put on the new man which was created according to God, in righteousness and holiness' (Eph 4:24). This sounds rather impossible, and it is impossible in the sense that you will try in vain to do this yourself. Fortunately it is possible because the Holy Spirit can do this for you and in you. Ultimately you will radiate God's glory in your life. People looking at you will see this glory radiating from you.

The Spirit will let you do three things to bring about this metamorphosis in you:

- When the Spirit works in you, you will want to give up your old way of life – you will want to break free from the old sinful person with whom you have been living for so long.
- You will start thinking in a new way – from now on your thoughts will be more directed at the things of God.
- You will be prepared to cultivate new habits – habits which are in line with the way Jesus lived, spoke and acted.

Total Surrender

God does not see as man sees. Jesus looks at your heart. True metamorphosis requires a change of heart. You should also realise that all inner change is God's work; it is done by the power of the Holy Spirit and we can therefore take no credit for it. If you are prepared to obey the voice of the Holy Spirit, this type of change is not impossible or even difficult. Turn to listen to the voice of the Holy Spirit like the sails of a yacht are filled by the wind, and allow God to change you, to make you more and more like His Son.

'Conforming to Christ is not the result of imitating, but of surrendering,' Rick Warren writes. Sanctification therefore involves that you will be prepared to surrender yourself totally to God. He is not interested in only part of you; He wants all of you. You will have to be willing to surrender everything which identifies you as you. You will have to be willing to live according to God's plan. Paul says, 'Be transformed by the renewing of your mind, that you may prove what is that good and acceptable and perfect will of God' (Rom 12:2). Therefore, allow God to change you and turn you into a totally new creature.

This process of total transformation will continue all your life. It might not be very easy, but will have much greater dividends for you than you could ever imagine. Do not hesitate any longer to accept God's offer!

Lord Jesus,

forgive me for having resisted
your changing my life for so long.
Please change me day by day
until I will ultimately be like You;
until I will no longer live,
but You will live in me ...
Start with my heart; change my thoughts,
my way of life and the things I say.
Make me a new person,
so I can live completely according to your will
and be holy like You.
Make me willing to make a complete break with sin,
and help me to acquire the right habits,
to give myself totally to You,
until I will one day reflect your glory,
and so people will see You when they look at me.
I realise this is impossible unless your Spirit
works this metamorphosis in me.
Please change me, Lord.

The reason we need God, and a power from beyond ourselves, is that real change always flows from within. It is a matter of the heart. Inner change takes place in that hidden area of our lives which only God can reach and which we cannot see without God's help. It is God's Spirit alone who can bring about the change of heart that is our deepest need.

— Trevor Hudson

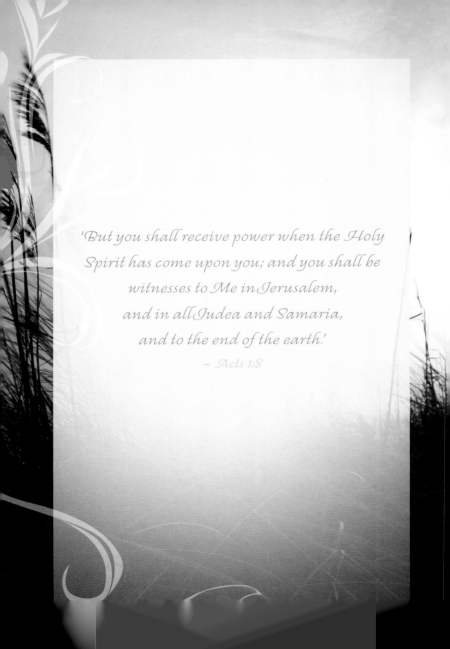

'But you shall receive power when the Holy
Spirit has come upon you; and you shall be
witnesses to Me in Jerusalem,
and in all Judea and Samaria,
and to the end of the earth.'

– Acts 1:8

Witness with a difference

All of Us Are Witnesses

Every Christian is inevitably a witness. After He was raised from the dead, Jesus sent his disciples out to be his witnesses, to win people to Him and to baptise them in his Name. God still asks this of his children. It should be practically impossible for us to remain silent about the wonder of our faith: 'For we cannot but speak the things which we have seen and heard,' Peter and John said when the Sanhedrin commanded them not to speak or teach about Jesus (Acts 4:20). God needs you as His witness in the world, to tell other people what He means to you.

Remember that witnessing does not merely consist of words, but also of deeds, and of the things you do not do and say.

A Witness with Impact

A report by a regular columnist who was for ever badmouthing Christians and their God appeared in the supplement, 'By', of *Die Burger* on Saturday, 18 August 2007. It was obvious that he had no interest in and attached no value to people who try to live according to Biblical guidelines. Week after week he received indignant SMS messages from Christians who accused him of being, inter alia, an 'empty-headed blasphemer of God'. One SMS message read: 'I dare you to put God to the test, if you have the courage'.

However, this same cynical columnist made a U-turn when he met someone — in a bar of all places. He calls this person 'Piet-Retief-of-Secunda'. Piet and our columnist chatted for quite a while, and during this chat something happened to the latter. He discovered that Piet Retief 'had a witness with a difference' to share. This Piet, unlike other Christians, made 'a lasting impression' (the columnist's own words) on him. According to the writer, this Piet Retief character looked like a tough guy, but talked like a man with a greater vision. As a child he had been abused by an alcoholic father and had been a *recce* during the Border war. After the war he had to try to sort himself out without any psychological assistance. He consequently gave vent to his aggression by trying to solve all his problems with his fists.

'God saved him,' our columnist wrote without even the slightest hint of his usual sarcasm. 'God calmed Piet-Retief-of-Secunda and turned him into a better person. God changed his life, saved his marriage, improved his relationship with his children and prevented him from reverting to the vicious cycle in which he had grown up.'

I read this article with growing amazement, but nothing prepared me for the conclusion.

'It was as if I had been struck by the blinding light on the road to Damascus,' the columnist testified. 'If he did not have God in his life, he would most probably have tackled me about the stuff I had written in the past, about things I had said, so that he could eventually have gone home and bragged in the bar about having beaten me up. But no, he knew how I felt about religion and accepted it as such. It did not prevent him from telling me how he felt about it. He was proud of his God and grateful for the peace He had brought into his life. His God is a living God who is present in his daily life; not Someone he merely honoured in a brick-and-mortar building on Sundays. Piet-Retief-from-Secunda made me think. I take my hat off to him.' (Quoted from 'By', Saturday, 18 August 2007.)

After I had read this article I felt like Moses at the burning bush. I wondered what our columnist's next article would be like; whether Piet's testimony-with-a-difference would have made a lasting impression on him, and whether it had given him a glimpse of this God for whom he had not spared a real thought up until then. I also wondered what I would have said to him if I had been the one he had been talking to. I have to admit that I would definitely have been aggressive and would therefore have achieved absolutely nothing.

Testify Carefully

Your testimony can back God, or alienate people from Him. Therefore, be careful about what you tell unbelievers about your God. Base your testimony on the testimony of Piet-Retief-from-Secunda in future so that it will not be judgemental in any way but filled with your love for and pride in the God you worship. And always remember: Testifying is God's work. You yourself cannot achieve anything by testifying, but if you are willing to allow God to speak through you, and furthermore live as if you know God, you cannot fail to touch people who look at your life and listen to your words. 'First live the gospel, and then speak about it,' writes Henrietta Mears. This is the very best advice about how to win other people to God.

147

Heavenly Father,

I try so hard, yet I fail so often
when I want to testify about You.
I am so aware of myself and my own shortcomings
that I forget that You are there to assist me.
Teach me to be a witness
who is totally dependent on You;
someone who relies on the power of your Holy Spirit.
Thank you for the promise
that You Yourself will give me the right words
at exactly the right moment.
Make me a careful witness,
so that I will not alienate other people
with my sharp words or negative attitude,
and help me to act in such a way
that my whole life will underline
and supportmy testimony.

As a witness you have to remain
intensely dependent on the Lord,
because you know that you yourself
cannot give people the right answers.
You only realise that you are fully dependent
on the Holy Spirit for what you say
and for the testimony of your life
once you realise that you are handing the
words of life to other people like bread.

— Johan van Schalkwyk

The LORD will command His loving
kindness in the daytime, and in the night
His song shall be with me— A prayer to the
God of my life.

– Psalm 42:8

Make Music with Everything in You

A friend who is living in Portugal at the moment sent me an exceptional e-mail about the violinist Itzhak Perlman. Perlman had polio as a child and it's always difficult for him to cross the stage to his chair carrying his violin. He uses crutches and wears callipers on both legs. When he reaches his chair, he puts his crutches on the floor, bends down and removes the callipers, and only then he picks up his violin, places it under his chin and starts playing.

One night while Perlman was performing with a symphony orchestra in New York, one of the violin strings snapped audibly. The audience waited in silence for him to pick up the callipers and put them on, take up his crutches and leave the stage. However, Perlman closed his eyes for a brief moment and then indicated to the conductor to continue. The orchestra started again and Itzhak continued where he had stopped. He played with even more passion and purity than before on his violin — which had only three strings left. Most people in the audience knew that it was impossible to try to play a symphony on a violin with only three strings, but that night Itzhak Perlman refused to acknowledge the 'fact'. He practically had to 'rewrite' the whole violin concerto in his mind to be able to do this — and when he finished there was a deathly hush in the concert hall. Then the audience rose to their feet and gave him a standing ovation which lasted several minutes. Perlman smiled, wiped the beads of perspiration from his forehead, lifted his bow in acknowledgement and to calm the audience, and said: 'You know, sometimes it's the artist's task to discover how much music you can still make with what you have left.'

A Song in the Night

'Perhaps this is the true definition of life,' was the concluding sentence of my e-mail. 'No, not only for artists, but for each one of us. Here was a man who had practised violin music on a violin with four strings all his life, and suddenly he discovered in the middle of a violin concerto that he only had three strings left. He used those three strings to make music which was more beautiful, more holy, more unforgettable than any music he had ever made before. Therefore, perhaps it's our task in this wavering, rapidly changing incomprehensible world in which we live to make music too – at first with everything we have and then – when this is no longer possible – to make music with everything we have left.'

What makes this e-mail even more special to me is the fact that the friend who had sent it is a very gifted harpist who gives recitals in Portugal. She was diagnosed with breast cancer a year ago, but despite severe chemotherapy and radiation treatment she has continued her recitals and has touched many people's hearts with the beauty of her music.

'People say I play the cello with the ease of a bird in flight. I do not know how much effort a bird puts into learning to fly, but I do know how much incredibly hard work every cello performance requires of me,' the famous cello virtuoso, Pablo Casals, once said.

We all know that it's not always easy to make music. As in the case of Itzhak Perlman, it always requires that the artist gives his or her very best. It requires an incredibly severe practise programme if you want to develop your musical talent fully.

Do not allow problems in your life to prevent you from making music; from singing to God a song with your life, even at night. You have the assurance that God will never let you go. He remains faithful, even when you sometimes become unfaithful. This 'music' created in times of suffering is often more beautiful and melodious than ever before.

Heavenly Father,

today I want to ask You to enable me to sing You a song
even when I am surrounded by darkness;
to look to You when my feet are slipping
so that your faithful love can help me to remain standing;
to find peace in your comforting when I am struggling
against huge anxiety in my heart.
I praise You for your faithfulness,
even when I am at times unfaithful to You.
Thank you that I may know that You
will always help me again.
I would like to continue making music
unto You with all I have and,
when this is no longer possible because
of difficult circumstances,
to make music with everything I have left.
Let this music in the midst of suffering be more sincere,
more beautiful and more passionate than ever before.
Please enable me to do this.

Eighty years ago I began my day in the
same way ... I awaken, and I go to the piano
and play two preludes and a fugue from Bach.
These pieces function as a
blessing upon my house. But this practice is
also a way of reestablishing
contact with the mystery of life and with
the miracle of being a human being.
Even though I've done this for eighty years,
the music is never the same — it always teaches
me something new fantastic, unbelievable.

— Pablo Casals

For I know the thoughts that I think toward you, says the LORD, thoughts of peace and not of evil, to give you a future and a hope. Then you will call upon Me and go and pray to Me, and I will listen to you.

– Jeremiah 29:11–12

Seven Principles to Enrich Your Life

God's children can testify with the prophet Jeremiah that God plans prosperity for them, and that He will give them a future, an expectation. However, we can implement many things personally to enrich our lives. In his book *Your Best Life Now,* Joel Osteen discusses seven of these principles. The following is a brief summary of his ideas on each of these principles:

1. Enlarge Your Vision

If your thoughts can change, God will change your life. If you think you cannot do something, you are right. If you think you can do it, you are also right. Therefore, learn to think big! You have to replace your negative thoughts with positive ones before you can change your life positively, because your life always follows your expectations. Expect, therefore, that all will be well, and it will be. Remember that God can still do far more than you can pray or think! (see Ephesians 3:20). Find a dream for yourself and work towards it until it is realised. If you are willing to persevere, God Himself will open the necessary doors for you.

2. Develop a Healthy Self-Image

You should base your self-image on what the Bible says about you, and not what you think about yourself. If you have regarded yourself as unqualified, unattractive, inferior and inadequate to date, all other people probably think likewise. However, this is not what God thinks of you at all. To Him you are precious, because He loves you and has created you in his own image. You can change your poor self-image by beginning to agree with God. Instead of focusing on your weaknesses, you can focus on God and believe that you are able to do all things through Him who strengthens you (see Philippians 4:13). See yourself as a winner, as God sees you. Believe that God will do great things for you — nothing is impossible for Him. Think positively and be happy about who you are.

3. Discover the Power of Your Thoughts and Words

Your thoughts and feelings are close together. You will never feel good about yourself unless you think positively about yourself. Choose therefore to set your mind on 'the things above' (Col 3:2). God will change your whole life positively if you are prepared to think positively. 'God created you and He has programmed you for victory,' Osteen writes.

The things you say are as powerful as your thoughts. If things go wrong and you only say negative things (like many people do about our own government and the situation in our country at the moment), those circumstances will never improve. It is far better to be positive, to speak words of faith and victory. Your words have a tremendous effect on yourself and those around you.

4. Let Go of the Past

Like Paul you should forget what lies behind. Remember that God wants to give you a future, an expectation, and reach out to the future with the sure knowledge that God loves you. Then refuse to allow negative things of the past to make you bitter. Forgive those who were responsible for the failures in your past and focus on the future (see Jeremiah 29:11). Osteen makes the interesting observation that, although forgiveness is a choice, it is not an option. God expects you to forgive others as He is always prepared to forgive you. Instead of tackling things yourself and setting them right, allow God to do this for you. You will still experience disappointments, but believe that God will make all things work together for your good in the future.

5. Find Strength through Adversity

Trust God to help you, but be prepared to wait on Him. Allow God to answer your prayers in his own time and way. It's particularly in times of crisis that you discover the stuff you are made of; it is then that your true strength comes to the fore. Your faith is tested in times of crisis. Even if God does not always change your circumstances, He changes you for the better when you are battling. Therefore, never give up, but trust God, even when nothing is making sense to you.

6. Live to Give!

Christians should learn to live unselfishly, to see the need of others and do something about it. Like Jesus when He was on earth, you really have to care for others so that they can experience the love and empathy of God through your conduct. Be generous and give more than you can afford. People who give generously receive abundant blessings from God.

7. Choose to be Happy

Happiness is always a choice; it is a decision you make, not an emotion you feel. Choose every morning to be positive and happy that day. Learn to notice small things which can fill you with joy; stop regretting things you cannot change. Blossom where you have been planted and appreciate everything God gives you rather than always wanting more. Be the very best person you can be, and never sacrifice your integrity; be enthusiastic about everything and you will soon see how your life will change positively.

If you comply with Joel Osteen's principles every day, you will soon notice positive results in your own life.

Heavenly Father,

how wonderful to know that You are on my side;
that You are planning prosperity for me
and that You want to give me an expectation.
Teach me to enrich my life by enlarging my vision,
developing a sound self-image,
and by taking note of what You think of me.
From now on I want to see to it
that my thoughts and my words
will always be positive and edifying
I want to put the failures of the past behind me
and even use my adversity to become a stronger person.
Help me not to be selfish, but that, in future,
I will choose to be truly happy every day,
because I trust You with my whole life.

We can only make our world a happier place if we ourselves first learn to be happy in our own hearts. We set out on this learning journey when we develop reasonable expectations with regard to happiness, start to take responsibility for the way we respond to life, and allow God to really be God in our lives.

– Trevor Hudson

Keep your heart with all diligence,
for out of it spring the issues of life.
Death and life are in the power of
the tongue, and those who
love it will eat its fruit.

– Proverbs 4:23; 18:21

The Power of Words

People Come to Know You By Your Words

Of all the creatures God has made, only man can communicate by means of words. By means of words you verbalise your love for others, but words can also hurt. The version of Proverbs 18:21 in The Message reads as follows: 'Words kill, words give life; they're either poison or fruit — you choose'. The saying, *the pen is more powerful than the sword,* is very true. Most people do not realise the power inherent in their words. By means of your words you can make people happy, raise them up or encourage them, but your words can also hurt and run them down. Words must therefore be used very carefully, because people come to know you by your words; your words convey to them the language of your heart. Jesus Himself says, 'Out of the abundance of the heart the mouth speaks. A good man out of the good treasure of his heart brings forth good things, and an evil man out of the evil treasure brings forth evil things' (Matt 12:34b—35).

The ease with which modern man uses dirty words, crude words, expletives and curses is disconcerting. It has become so much part of the language of some people that they no longer even notice it. Expletives and curses are used in such a 'natural' way in books, films and television programmes, that young children are unfortunately getting used to them.

The Pleasure of Words

Some words are so wonderful that you have to put them away in your memory box to be taken out and enjoyed over and over again. I will never forget when, at eighteen months, my granddaughter called me 'Ou-ma Ni-na' for the first time — with a broad smile! And I enjoy it as much when her mom wants her to do something against her will and she calls anxiously, 'Ninaaaaa!'

I have loved words from an early age and have been collecting words and quotations which I like since childhood. My husband is a creative writer of high calibre and one of the things which actually made me notice him initially was the way he used words.

Guard Against Using Your Words as Weapons

When you are very angry, hurtful words slip out very easily. And unfortunately once spoken, it is impossible to take words back. 'Be gentle and graceful with your words,' writes Phil Bosmans. 'Words should be lights. Words should reconcile, bring together, make peace. When words become weapons, people are in opposition as enemies. Life is far too short and our world far too small to turn them into a battlefield.'

Your words can hurt others in three ways: when you gossip about them, when you tell lies (and even the truth) about them, and when you say hurtful things about them in their presence. Stop saying things about others when you are not sure of the facts, or if you lack the boldness to say the same things to their faces.

Your Words Remain Forever

One of the most frightening characteristics of words is that once spoken a word can never become unsaid again. In his book *The Hermit,* Ebba Pauli tells the story of a very unpopular woman who wanted to know from him why nobody liked her. The hermit then gave the woman a flower with very fine little seeds and asked her to blow on them. When she did so, the light seeds became airborne and after a short while they dropped down on the ground. 'Now pick up all the seeds,' the hermit told the woman. 'I can't,' she protested. 'You cannot even see them any longer. Who knows where they have fallen now?' 'Yes,' the hermit said, 'who can know where they have fallen? It is just as impossible to gather the words you drop among people. They remain where they have fallen, and they grow like these seeds will now grow.'

No matter how you regret your sharp words, nothing you can do will ever make those words unsaid again. And the person to whom you said those hurtful words may perhaps forgive you, but he or she will probably never forget those words.

Be sure to consider your words in future and weigh them before you say them so that your words will be a blessing to others. It is my wish that the words in Psalm 19:14 will always be true about you: 'Let the words of my mouth and the meditation of my heart be acceptable in Your sight, O LORD, my Strength and my Redeemer.'

Lord,

thank you that I could once again discover
the tremendous power hidden in my words.
You know that I fail most often
in the area of my words.
I love talking and I talk so much
that I often do not realise the tremendous damage
I do with my words.
Make me less talkative and more sensitive.
Forgive me for all the times when my words
were weapons with which I hurt people.
Help me to use words much more carefully in future.
Please prevent me from hurting people with my words.
Give me your words of blessing
so that I can encourage others with them.
I would like your words to remain in me.

Guard against being judgemental.
Words are powerful weapons
which can do much harm.
Don't use your big mouth
to make someone else small.
Turn your heart into an oasis for
people so that your words can be the
water which makes deserts fertile.
The word is a miraculous gift which
God has given mankind
so that they can form a community.
Words must never be a weapon.
Let God live in your word,
and your word will be:
light, love and life.

– Phil Bosmans

And when they [the magi] had come into the house, they saw the young Child with Mary His mother, and fell down and worshiped Him. And when they had opened their treasures, they presented gifts to Him: gold, frankincense, and myrrh.

– Matthew 2:11

The Legend of the Magi

According to tradition, the legend of the three astrologers was recorded by Marco Polo on his journeys to China in the thirteenth century and brought back to Venice: Caspar, the king of Tarsus, was young, tall and black as ebony. Belshazzar, the king of Chaldea, was middle-aged, of average height with an olive skin. Melchior, the king of Nubia, was very old, bent and very pale. The three magi had followed the bright star in search of the new King who had been born.

The young Caspar felt the world needed a new King. He showed the other two the gift he had brought: gold for a king. Belshazzar, the middle-aged monarch, believed that a worldly king would not be enough — he wanted a revelation from God Himself and therefore he had brought the new King frankincense, which personified worship.

Melchior, who knew he was nearing the end of his life, was looking for a Redeemer — he knew instinctively that this Redeemer would have to suffer, and he therefore brought Him myrrh as a gift.

When they eventually arrived in Bethlehem, the three were extremely disappointed to find a newborn baby in his mother's arms — and then they heard the song she was singing:

'I praise the glory of the Lord...'

'The Lord!' Caspar called out. 'I have found the King!' — and he put his gift of gold before the Child worshipfully.

Mary's song continued:

'I glorify God ...'

'God!' Belshazzar said filled with emotion, 'My search has ended!' And he also put his gift of frankincense at the Child's little feet.

'... my Redeemer,' Mary continued singing.

'My Redeemer!' repeated Melchior gratefully. And he took out his gift of myrrh and laid it at the feet of the young Child.

So Caspar found the King he had been searching for, Belshazzar found the God he had been looking for and Melchior found the Redeemer who could satisfy his deepest needs.

The Meeting of Our Needs

To those who know and love Him, Jesus is still the realisation of their deepest desires. He is the only one Who can unlock the door to heaven for us, Who guarantees by his death on the cross that every fraction of our sin has been paid for so that God can forgive us. Yet while He was on earth He was completely human so that He now knows the needs of human beings in detail and can share in all our suffering and joy. Small wonder that John Bunyan testified many years ago that 'Christ is the heart's desire of nations, the joy of the angels, the apple of the Father's eye. How wonderful it must be for everyone in whose spirit He lives for all eternity!' If you have Jesus in your life, you know that no-one can ever snatch you from his hand, and you also know you need nothing else!

Lord Jesus,

I want to kneel down before You
and worship You like the magi of old —
You are the fulfilment of all my needs and desires,
You are my Lord, my God and my Redeemer —
You are my heart's desire and You give me all my joy.
It's so wonderful to know that You
chose me to belong to You.
When I consider everything You did for me —
that You even left heaven to come into the world
as an ordinary human being for my sake,
to live and suffer here so that I could be redeemed —
I want to show You my gratitude.
I want to entrust my whole life to You
and praise and honour and serve You for the rest of my life.
I also want to tell others what You mean to me.
Make me holy, Lord, so that I will become
more like You every day.

Jesus Christ does not want to be our helper;
He wants to be our life, He does not want
us to work for Him, He wants us to let Him
do His work through us, using us, as we use a
pencil to write with – better still, using us
as one of the fingers ons His hand.

– Charles G Trumbull

May the LORD our God be with us,
as He was with our fathers. May He
not leave us nor forsake us, that He
may incline our hearts to Himself, to
walk in all His ways, and to keep His
commandments and His statutes
and His judgments, which He
commanded our fathers ... Let your heart
therefore be loyal to the LORD our God,
to walk in His statutes and keep His
commandments, as at this day.

— 1 Kings 8: 57–58, 61

Is God On His Way Out?

The beautiful story of how the Ark of the Lord was placed in the temple is told in 1 Kings 8. At the dedication of the temple Solomon blessed the people and prayed to God. All Israel brought sacrifices and Solomon sacrificed 22 000 bulls and 120 000 sheep to the Lord! 'So the king and all the children of Israel dedicated the house of the LORD,' verse 63 reads. Verses 10 and 11 read, 'And it came to pass, when the priests came out of the holy place, that the cloud filled the house of the LORD, so that the priests could not continue ministering because of the cloud; for the glory of the LORD filled the house of the LORD.'

Paul also refers to the glory of the Lord. He says that God's glory should fill the lives of God's children so that it will radiate from their lives. Writing to the Corinthian church he says, 'We all, with unveiled face, beholding as in a mirror the glory of the Lord, are being transformed into the same image from glory to glory, just as by the Spirit of the Lord' (2 Cor 3:18).

The Holy Spirit Lives in You

Some people are so radiant with the joy of the Lord that you cannot help but notice it. This lasting joy is available to everybody. In the above verse, Paul says that we are being transformed into his very own image from one degree of glory to another. He then adds, 'for this comes from the Lord [Who is] the Spirit' (AMP). Without the Holy Spirit in your life you will struggle in vain to reflect the glory of the Lord. The closer you live to the Holy Spirit, the greater his sovereignty in your life and the more visible God's glory will be in your life.

All God's children are temples of the Holy Spirit and the presence of the Lord should be visible in our lives. We should be temples where the Holy Spirit wants to dwell. 'Do you not know that you are the temple of God and that the Spirit of God dwells in you? … Do you not know that your body is the temple of the Holy Spirit Who is in you?' Paul asks the Corinthian church (1 Cor 3:16; 6:19a), 'Do you not know that your body is the temple of the Holy Spirit Who lives within you, Whom you have received [as a gift] from God? You are not your own, you were bought for a price … So then, honor God and bring glory to Him in your body,' he adds (1 Cor 6:19b–20, AMP).

If you are serious about your calling as a Christian, Solomon's prayer will be fulfilled in your life and the glory of God will fill your 'temple' every day of your life.

When God Withdraws

However, the Bible warns repeatedly that if we remain disobedient to God, the Lord will withdraw his presence from us. At the beginning of the book Ezekiel, the prophet meets

God in the forecourt of the temple, because God's presence was leaving — this time God was leaving the temple. Once this happened the temple would no longer be God's sanctuary but merely an ordinary building.

God's people had disobeyed Him once too often and they were to be taken away as exiles. At the end of the book, however, this same God gave Ezekiel a message of hope for God's people. He gave Ezekiel a vision of a new temple, a temple where God would live among his people forever. In 537 BC Babylon was seized by King Cyrus and he allowed the Jewish people to return to their country so that God's promise to Ezekiel could be fulfilled.

A Personal Warning

The warning that God's patience with us — with you, too — could run out, should be taken very personally. If you are repeatedly disobedient to God or refuse to listen to Him, God could withdraw from your life. However, this will only happen if you withdraw from Him first. Israel was carried away to Babylon as a result of their persistent disobedience to God, but during their captivity they once again started reading the Scriptures and subsequently returned to their God. God heard their prayers, forgave their sin and brought them back to their country.

The Lord is always prepared to take you back, to give you another chance if you want to return to Him.

Lord,

I'm so sure that You are present in my life,
that I am a temple of Your Holy Spirit —
yet I realise that I sometimes still wander away from You,
that I disappoint You like your people so long ago.
Thank you for being so patient with me.
Help me to be faithful to You,
so that I will always radiate your glory.
Please let your glory will increase in my life
so that it will be visible to others.
Help me to live according to your will
and to obey your commandments,
so that I will be able to live fully surrendered to You.
I know I cannot do this on my own,
but that I need the Holy Spirit
to pour out your glory in my life.

As the sun, which would shine
in its own brightness and glory though all
the world were blind, or did wilfully shut
their eyes against it, so God will be ever
most glorious, let men be ever so obstinate
or rebellious. Yea, God will have glory by
reprobates, though it be nothing to their ease;
and though He be not glorified of them,
yet He will glorify Himself in them.

– N Rodgers

Bibliography

Auclair, Marcelle. *Die kuns om gelukkig te wees* (Christelike Uitgewersmaatskappy, Vereeniging: 1988)

Campolo, Tony: *You Can Make a Difference* (W Publishing Group, Nashville, Tennessee: 1984)

De Pree, Max. *Letters to My Miracle Grandchild* (Harper Collins, New York: 1999)

Groot Aanhalingsboek, Die (Lux Verbi.BM, Wellington: 2004)

Eareckson-Tada, Joni. *Glorious Intruder* (Multnomah Press, Oregon: 1989)

Heyns, Johan. *Wie dieper delf* (Nasionale Boekhandel, Cape Town: 1968)

Jones, Brian. *Second Guessing God.* (Standard Publishing , Cincinnati: 2006)

Kierkegaard, Sören. *Philosophical Fragments* (Princeton University Press, New Jersey: 1974)

L'Engle, Madeleine. *Glimpses of Grace* (Harper Collins, New York: 1996)

Lewis, CS. *Doodgewoon Christen* (Lux Verbi.BM, Wellington: 2007)

Mandino, Og. *The Greatest Secret in the World* (Bantam Books , New York: 1972)

Ortberg, John. *Everybody's Normal Till You Get to Know Them* (Zondervan, Michigan: 2003)

Ortberg, John. *Love Beyond Reason* (Zondervan, Michigan: 1998)

Ortberg, John. *The Life You've Always Wanted* (Zondervan, Michigan: 1997)

Ortberg, John. *God Is Closer Than You Think* (Zondervan, Michigan: 2005)

Ortberg, John. *When The Game Is Over, It All Goes Back in the Box* (Zondervan, Michigan: 2007)

Osteen, Joel. *Your Best Life* Now (FaithWords, New York: 2001)

Pauli, Ebba. *Die Kluisenaar* (JL van Schaik, Pretoria: 1983)

Scheepers, Riana. *'n Engel in my huis* (Protea Boekehuis, Hatfield: 2005)

Smit, Johan. *Gebed, 'n omvattende gids* (Christelike Uitgewersmaatskappy, Vereeniging: 2007)

Smit, Johan. *Leef vir Christus* (Struik Christian Books, Cape Town: 1992)

Smit, Nina. *Groot Boek van Christelike Aanhalings* (Christelike Uitgewersmaatskappy, Vereeniging: 2005)

Smit, Nina. *Groot Boek van Christelike Aanhalings Volume 2* (Christelike Uitgewersmaatskappy, Vereeniging: 2008)

Smith, Stephen W. *Embracing Soul Care* (Kregel Publications, Grand Rapids: 2006)

Warren, Rick. *Purpose-Driven Life, The* (Zondervan Publishers, Grand Rapids, Michigan: 2002)

Watson, Lilian Eichler. *Light from Many Lamps* (Simon and Schuster, New York: 1951)

Wiid, Annalise. *Abjater is 'n kuierkat* (Perskor, Doornfontein: 1995)

Yancey, Philip. *Prayer* (Zondervan, Michigan: 2007)

We would like to hear from you.
Please send your comments about this book to us at:
reviews@struikchristianmedia.co.za

STRUIK CHRISTIAN GIFTS

BEAUTY. PASSION.
INSPIRATION.

www.struikchristianmedia.co.za